EYEWITNESS
FIRST LADIES

Written by
AMY PASTAN

In Association with the

Smithsonian

Jacqueline Kennedy's
Graflex camera

Mamie
Eisenhower
piggy bank

Frances Cleveland plate

Grace Coolidge's Native
American bracelet

Martha Washington's trunk

Abigail Adams's
embroidered shoes

Clinton campaign button

Martha Washington States china

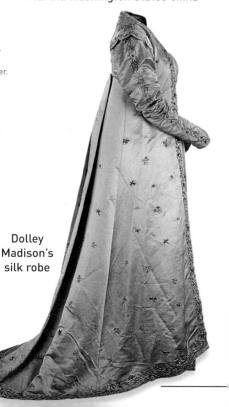

Dolley
Madison's
silk robe

DK | Penguin Random House

Editor Andrea Curley   Designer Jane Horne
Senior Art Editor Michelle Baxter
Art Director Tina Vaughan   Publisher Andrew Berkhut
Production Director David Proffit

SECOND EDITION
Editor John Searcy   Publishing Director Beth Sutinis
Designers Jessica Park, Bill Miller, Danielle Delaney
Jacket Designer Andrew Smith   CD Designer Sunita Gahir
Managing Art Editor Michelle Baxter
Production Controller Jen Lockwood
DTP Designer Kathy Farias

THIRD EDITION
Senior Editor Rebecca Warren   Editorial Director Nancy Ellwood
Assistant Managing Editor Allison Singer   Designer Jessica Park
Production Controller Jimmy Lao

RELAUNCH EDITION
DK US
Editor Jenny Siklos   Senior Editor Margaret Parrish
Additional Text Margaret Parrish   Editorial Director Nancy Ellwood

DK INDIA
Assistant Art Editor Nidhi Rastogi   DTP Designer Pawan Kumar
Senior DTP Designer Harish Aggarwal
Picture Researcher Sakshi Saluja   Jacket Designer Garima Sharma
Managing Editor Kingshuk Ghoshal   Managing Art Editor Govind Mittal

DK UK
Senior Art Editor Spencer Holbrook   Jacket Editor Claire Gell
Jacket Design Development Manager Sophia MTT
Producer, pre-production Jacqueline Street   Producer Vivienne Yong
Managing Editor Francesca Baines   Managing Art Editor Philip Letsu
Publisher Andrew Macintyre   Associate Publishing Director Liz Wheeler
Art Director Karen Self   Design Director Phil Ormerod
Publishing Director Jonathan Metcalf

First American Edition, 2001
This edition published in the United States in 2017 by
DK Publishing, 345 Hudson Street, New York, New York 10014

A WORLD OF IDEAS:
SEE ALL THERE IS TO KNOW

www.dk.com

Contents

Rosalynn Carter's purse

Martha Washington

America's initial first lady preferred managing an estate to fighting political battles. Martha's first husband died, leaving her with two small children. During the Revolutionary War (1775 to 1783), she accompanied her second husband, General George Washington, to the camps, and was admired for her patriotism. Martha was a grandmother when Washington became president of the new American democracy in 1789. Known as "Lady Washington," she preferred a less noble title, but understood that she was a role model for women.

Martha was not fond of political life, but she respected her husband for "obeying the voice of his country"

Brocade fabric

Sewn with care
Martha Washington was known for her needlework. A note left by her granddaughter Eliza Parke Custis states that "this Quilt was entirely the work of my Grandmother as far as the plain borders. I finish'd it in 1815 & leave it to my Rosebud." Rosebud was Eliza's daughter, Eliza L. Rogers. Martha kept her needles in this case (above left).

Reluctant correspondent
Martha had little education. She learned how to read and write in order to communicate with her family when she moved away.

Revolutionary wives

Women had a large role in the Revolutionary War. Martha Washington's contribution during this period is well known because her husband was commander in chief of the colonial army before becoming president. Risking her own safety, Martha traveled far from her home to visit General Washington. While at his camps, she tended the sick and saw to her husband's needs. Mrs. Washington was not the only wife who followed her husband in the war. Other wives also traveled to wash and mend clothing and cook food. Some even took a spouse's place in battle if he was wounded.

Martha Washington's expense report

A dashing suitor
Martha's first husband's death left her a wealthy widow. Though she had many suitors, she was impressed by George Washington, who had fought Indian wars in the West and was active in Virginia politics. After marrying him in 1759, Martha, with her young children, Patsy and Jacky, moved to his home at Mount Vernon in Virginia. She led the life of an 18th-century wife by helping his career and managing their household.

Army wife
When Martha visited General Washington in the field, she probably would have seen him planning his battle strategies in this tent (above).

Reporting a lady's travels
From 1775 to 1782, Martha weathered many harsh winters to see George, and he would later report her travel expenses (above).

On the go
Throughout the Revolutionary War, Martha packed and repacked her belongings in this trunk. Her trips to military sites up and down the East Coast were long, uncomfortable, and dangerous. Not all colonists supported independence from Great Britain.

Relief efforts
Mrs. Washington visited soldiers at Newburgh on Hudson, New York, in 1782. Martha helped improve the comfort and morale of the troops by mending uniforms and knitting wool garments. She led relief efforts for soldiers by organizing women to raise funds and roll bandages.

Hostess for the nation

After George Washington became president in 1789, the Washingtons moved to New York City, the first capital of the US. Martha continued to oversee the household in their rented home on Broadway. Mrs. Washington was careful not to behave like royalty. Guests were often invited to their home for dinner parties and receptions, and to "drawing rooms," which were more relaxed gatherings.

Dinner invitation

Design of flowers and insects

Bustle

Eighteenth-century style
Fashionable dresses of the 1780s had a front bodice, a full skirt, and a bustle. Mrs. Washington's elegant silk gown is painted with floral bouquets and insects—popular themes of the time.

Symbol of an unbreakable bond
Martha's most prized china had a pattern with each state—there were 15 at the time—bound by a strong chain (right).

State names

Chain symbolizing the strength of the new nation

Martha Washington's initials

Setting an elegant table
Entertaining was a large part of life for the Washingtons. This bowl (above) is part of a set of Chinese porcelain dishes that were often used for elaborate meals. Mrs. Washington called herself an "old-fashioned Virginia house-keeper," but many guests admired the Washingtons' refined hospitality.

★ Martha Dandridge Custis Washington

PRESIDENT
George Washington

YEARS AS FIRST LADY
1789–1797

BORN
June 2, 1731
New Kent County, Virginia

MARRIED
January 6, 1759
Kent County, Virginia

CHILDREN FROM FORMER MARRIAGE
John Parke Custis
Martha Parke Custis

DIED
Age 70
May 22, 1802
Mount Vernon, Virginia

Eleanor Parke Custis

George Washington Parke Custis

Viewing the capital city
The Washingtons never lived in Washington, D.C., during George's years as president, though the site for the future federal city had been chosen. This artist's print shows Martha pointing to a map of the capital while her grandchildren—Eleanor and George, the children of Martha's son, John—look on.

Cupola with "dove of peace" weathervane

"Bull's-eye" window

Mount Vernon

Home to Virginia

After leaving the presidency in 1797, the Washingtons retired to Mount Vernon, their beloved home on the Potomac River in Virginia. Washington was 20 years old when he acquired the plantation, and he expanded the estate to eight thousand acres. A gentleman farmer, he rode 25 miles on horseback each day to inspect his fields. Martha managed a busy household that hosted hundreds of visitors yearly. This may not have been the quiet life Martha hoped for, but she welcomed invited guests and travelers who stopped for a glimpse of the man who had become a living legend.

Gilt-and-lacquered finish

Much of the fine furniture used by the Washingtons has survived to this day

Treasured gift

The Count de Custine-Sarreck, who served with French forces in America during the Revolutionary War, gave the Washingtons a set of porcelain dinnerware. Martha used this pitcher (left) at Mount Vernon and gave pieces of the porcelain to friends and family as mementos.

George Washington's initials in the center

Unbearable loss

In 1799, George Washington developed a throat infection and died of it on December 14, at the age of 67. After his death, his wife retreated to an attic chamber in their home. She could not bear to remain in their bedroom.

A flair for style

In the 18th century, men usually dealt with purchasing agents in Europe, so George may have ordered many pieces of furniture for Martha. She kept her jewelry in this dressing case (above).

Abigail Adams

Abigail Adams was the wife of one president and the mother of another: John Quincy Adams. A minister's daughter, she was taught at home like most girls of her time. Her intelligence, love of learning, and interest in politics made her the perfect partner for lawyer and politician John Adams. She is one of the few first ladies famous for her own accomplishments rather than for her husband's. During the Revolutionary War, Mrs. Adams ran their farm as canon fire erupted close by. She was a patriot who supported and influenced her husband strongly.

Happy partnership
Although John Adams was proud, vain, and stubborn, his wife was his supporter during a 50-year marriage. As his popularity as president waned, Abigail never failed to defend her husband against those who mocked his aristocratic style.

Abigail, shown in this artwork at age 56, spoke her mind and inspired future first ladies to take an active role in politics

A token of love
John Adams spent much of his career traveling within and outside of the US. In 1778, he went to Paris to serve as US minister of France. Before he left, he gave his wife this locket (right).

Inscription reading "I yield whatever is, is right"

My friend...
Over two thousand of Abigail Adams's letters have been preserved. Eloquent and witty, they discuss the major events of the Revolutionary War era.

"My Friend" of the salutation is John Adams

BUILDING THE FIRST WHITE HOUSE

WASHINGTON D.C. 1798

The president's house
Washington, D.C., became the country's capital in 1800, and the Adamses became the first family to live in what was then called the President's House. "The roads are said to be so bad," Abigail wrote, "the buildings so remote from each other that I fancy it will not be a residence much sought after for years to come."

Dress shoes
The embroidered shoes of yellow leather shown here are said to have belonged to Abigail Adams.

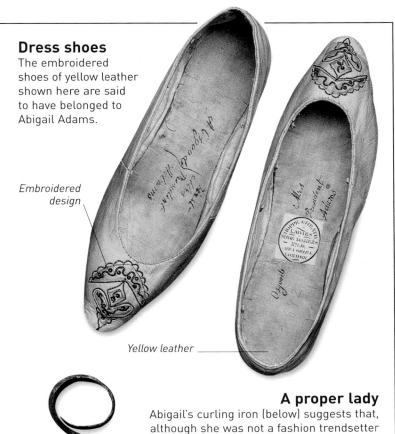

Embroidered design

Yellow leather

A proper lady
Abigail's curling iron (below) suggests that, although she was not a fashion trendsetter like some of the first ladies who succeeded her, she did give thought to her appearance.

Abigail Adams's curling iron

An unsuitable home for a first lady
In 1966, artist Gordon Phillips painted this imaginary scene of Mrs. Adams in the unfinished President's House. Abigail lamented, "We have not the least fence, yard, or other convenience... and the great unfinished audience-room I make a drying-room of, to hang up the clothes in."

Abigail Smith Adams

PRESIDENT
John Adams

YEARS AS FIRST LADY
1797–1801

BORN
November 23, 1744
Weymouth, Massachusetts

MARRIED
October 25, 1764
Weymouth, Massachusetts

CHILDREN
Abigail Amelia
John Quincy
Susanna
Charles
Thomas Boylston

DIED
Age 73
October 28, 1818
Quincy, Massachusetts

Martha Jefferson

Martha Skelton was a young and wealthy widow when she married a brilliant Virginia lawyer named Thomas Jefferson. Though little is known about Martha and no portraits of her exist, she and Jefferson both loved music and literature, and her husband later described his married life as "ten years of uncheckered happiness." Sadly, the difficult births of six children took their toll on Martha. She died at age 33—19 years before Jefferson became president in 1801. While president, Jefferson occasionally asked Dolley Madison, a family friend and future first lady, as well as his eldest daughter to preside over official festivities.

Grieving husband
Thomas Jefferson gained fame for writing the Declaration of Independence, but hoped to return to his Virginia estate after serving at the Continental Congress in Philadelphia in 1776. However, losing Martha "wiped away all my plans and left me a blank which I had not the spirits to fill up." Friends urged him to bury his grief and return to politics.

★

Martha Wayles Skelton Jefferson

PRESIDENT
Thomas Jefferson

YEARS AS FIRST LADY
Never served as first lady

BORN
October 30, 1748
Charles City County, Virginia

MARRIED
January 1, 1772
Charles City County, Virginia

CHILDREN
Martha
Maria
Lucy Elizabeth
Two girls and one boy
who died in infancy

DIED
Age 33
September 6, 1782
Charlottesville, Virginia

The top lifts to form a writing surface

Writing about liberty
The lap desk (right) on which Jefferson wrote the Declaration of Independence was designed by him and built by a Philadelphia cabinetmaker. Later, he gave the desk to his granddaughter as a wedding gift.

The drawer contained ink, quills, and other writing materials

Unidentified young man

President Thomas Jefferson

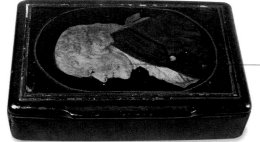

A popular image
Presidential portraits adorned objects during the 18th century, just like today. Jefferson's face is painted on this snuffbox (above). Snuff, a powder made of tobacco, was often used openly by men, but not by a refined woman.

Official hostess

After his wife's death, Thomas Jefferson relied on his oldest daughter, also named Martha. In 1784, she accompanied him to a diplomatic post in France, where she studied needlework, painting, history, and Latin at a convent school. At the time of this portrait, she was 51 years old and had 11 children.

The Jeffersons called this pitcher "the silver duck"

Martha Jefferson Randolph was nicknamed Patsy

The obelisk, an ancient Egyptian architectural form, is a tapered column topped by a pyramid

Invention and affection

A man of great ingenuity, Jefferson designed this clock (above). The face rests between two obelisks. He chose this shape for his grave marker years later. After his death, Martha Randolph wanted this object because it had been so close to her father.

Skelton silver

Martha Jefferson brought some possessions from her first marriage with her to Monticello. This silver spoon (right) was made in 1768 by Elizabeth Tookey of London.

Initials stand for Bathurst (Martha Jefferson's first husband) and Martha

Silver duck

The Jefferson family used this pitcher (above) as a chocolate pot at Monticello. Its shape was based on a Roman pouring vessel known as an askos.

Playtime at Monticello

This rare view of Monticello, painted in Jefferson's lifetime, shows one of Martha's children rolling a hoop with a stick. Two of Martha's daughters watch from the center of the garden.

George Wythe Randolph

Mary and Cornelia Randolph

Dolley Madison

Dolley Payne Todd married Virginia congressman James Madison less than a year after her first husband's death. By the time Madison became president, Dolley was an experienced political wife. Though her famous receptions were arranged to help her husband's career, she never favored one guest over another.

Revered first lady
Mrs. Madison was so highly thought of that a seat was reserved for her in the House of Representatives, an honor never before granted to any American woman.

By dawn's early light
The British bombardment of Fort McHenry inspired Francis Scott Key to compose a verse entitled "The Star-Spangled Banner." This later became the national anthem of the United States of America.

Saving the nation's heritage

When the US capital was attacked in the War of 1812, the first lady rescued valuable state documents from the President's House just before British troops set fire to it. This daring act, as well as her charm, won her the admiration of the American public. Her husband did not fare as well. After declaring war on Great Britain for harassing US ships, James was criticized for his inability to prevent the British from invading American shores.

The British are coming
During the War of 1812, 1,400 British soldiers burned and looted Washington. Dolley Madison kept calm and was undaunted by having to relocate temporarily. This painting is a modern artist's vision of that historic occasion.

A first lady rescues a general
Dolley saved this portrait of George Washington on August 24, 1814. Her servants broke the frame and rolled up the canvas, then carted it away in a wagon.

A capital hostess

Before becoming the first lady, Dolley was an occasional hostess for Thomas Jefferson. When she moved to the President's House, she was already respected as a leader of Washington society. The first lady blossomed in her new role. At Madison's inaugural ball, Dolley looked like a queen, with a purple bonnet with feathers. Her Wednesday evening receptions were open to all. After James's death, she remained an important figure in the social circles of the capital.

Dolley Payne Todd Madison

PRESIDENT
James Madison

YEARS AS FIRST LADY
1809–1817

BORN
May 20, 1768
Guilford County, North Carolina

MARRIED
September 15, 1794
Harewood, Virginia

CHILDREN FROM FORMER MARRIAGE
Payne Todd

DIED
Age 81
July 12, 1849
Washington, D.C.

Father of the Constitution
A serious, bookish, and soft-spoken man, James Madison brilliantly guided the writing of the US Constitution and fought for a Bill of Rights.

Embroidered design

Geometric designs

Satin splendor
Dolley wore this robe (left) after she left the President's House. The garment, with its raised waist, diamond-shaped back, and narrow sleeves, is fashionable for the 1820s. The silk satin is embroidered with butterflies, dragonflies, and phoenixes.

A dish for delightful desserts
This French porcelain (right) was used for Dolley's dazzling state dinners at the President's House. She was the first to serve ice cream there.

The incomparable Dolley Madison

Dolley had a warmth and vitality that drew people to her. At her funeral in 1849, President Taylor declared, "She will never be forgotten, because she was truly our first lady for a half-century." The term "first lady" stuck, and ultimately became the official title for the president's wife or official hostess.

Her own style
In this portrait, Dolley wears one of her distinctive turbans. Her spectacular clothes sometimes invited ridicule.

A gracious retirement home
After leaving the President's House, the Madisons retired to Montpelier. Dolley often had so many guests that tables had to be set up outside.

The lid is inscribed DPM

Just a pinch
This snuffbox (left) belonged to Dolley Madison. She was known to indulge in this habit, despite it being seen as unladylike.

Elizabeth Monroe

Although Elizabeth Monroe was shy and reserved, she played a key role in a diplomatic event while her husband, James, was serving as US minister to France after the French Revolution. During that turbulent period, the French executed supporters of their former king. This included the Marquis de Lafayette, a Frenchman who had helped Americans fight their own war for independence. Elizabeth dared to visit his wife in prison—and as a result, saved the patriot's wife from being beheaded.

A quiet first lady
Elizabeth did not attend many White House events, perhaps due to poor health. Women of Washington society disliked this because they could not attend an event if she was not there. This disturbed the social and political networks in the nation's capital.

A leader in good times
James Monroe was a popular president at a time of peace and tranquility, known as the Era of Good Feelings. He and Elizabeth had two daughters. One of them, Maria, had the first White House wedding.

Lafayette's daughters *Marquis de Lafayette* *Madame de Lafayette*

A daring rescue
The Marquis de Lafayette and his family were imprisoned in Paris because they were aristocrats. James Monroe felt that as an American diplomat, he could not directly help Madame de Lafayette, who was to be executed. Elizabeth went to the prison to see her, securing the noblewoman's release afterward.

The "White House"
During the War of 1812, the British had burned the Executive Mansion. By James Monroe's administration, the President's House was rebuilt and painted white. Thereafter it became known as the White House. Elizabeth brought a European elegance to her new home—learned when she and James lived in France.

Elizabeth Kortright Monroe

PRESIDENT
James Monroe

YEARS AS FIRST LADY
1817–1825

BORN
June 30, 1768
New York, New York

MARRIED
February 16, 1786
New York, New York

CHILDREN
Eliza
Maria Hester

DIED
Age 62
September 23, 1830
Oak Hill, Virginia

Louisa Adams

Louisa Adams disliked the duties of first lady, but rose to the task. Born in England to British and American parents, she realized that the diplomat she married was dour and inflexible. His disapproving mother, Abigail Adams, made matters worse. Yet her European manners made Louisa the most popular hostess in Washington. Louisa gave up on music for John's career, feeling she had no choice but to help her politically unpopular husband.

A passport to adventure
When John became US minister to Russia, Louisa entered St. Petersburg with this visa (above). When he was sent to Paris after the War of 1812, Louisa and her son Charlie traveled for 40 days across Europe in a sleigh in the winter.

An expensive plaything
It is unknown which of the children played with this rattle (above). It may have been George, who was born in London; John, born in Boston; Charles, born in Washington, D.C., or Louisa, who was born in Russia and died a year later.

A thwarted musician
Though she was a talented singer and harpist, Louisa had only one career option: to marry well and have children. She felt trapped in the White House, calling it "a dull and stately prison." Her journals reveal the frustrations of a woman whose talents could not flourish.

Unpopular president, difficult husband
A scholarly but serious, stubborn, and negative man, Adams lost his bid at reelection. Despite also being a difficult husband, he and his wife's relationship improved during his years in the House of Representatives.

Music in the White House
Before moving into the White House, Louisa played music for friends at gatherings. After becoming first lady, her husband asked her to stop. She did, however, host events where other musicians performed.

John Quincy Adams had a distinguished career as a member of Congress

---

⭐

Louisa Catherine Johnson Adams

PRESIDENT
John Quincy Adams

YEARS AS FIRST LADY
1825–1829

BORN
February 12, 1775
London, England

MARRIED
July 26, 1797
London, England

CHILDREN
George Washington
John
Charles Francis
Louisa Catherine

DIED
Age 77
May 15, 1852
Washington, D.C.

Rachel Jackson

In 1791, Rachel married Andrew Jackson, but discovered that her divorce from a previous abusive marriage had not yet been finalized. Though the situation was corrected, Rachel was sometimes accused of being a bigamist—a person with more than one legal spouse—to discredit Andrew.

Wronged Rachel
Being accused of bigamy was a vicious attack on a woman's morals—and the scandal took its toll. Rachel died of a heart attack five days after Jackson had won the election and become president.

Many talents
Andrew Jackson was a wealthy planter, judge, and military hero. Though a difficult man, he was a devoted husband who grieved deeply after Rachel's death.

Two Jackson hostesses
The Jacksons had no children of their own. In 1809, they adopted a nephew and named him Andrew Jackson Jr. Another nephew, Andrew Jackson Donelson, married Rachel's favorite niece, Emily. It was Emily whom the president asked to serve as hostess in the White House.

Portrait of Emily Donelson, by Ralph Earl, a friend of Jackson

Open house at the White House
Jackson's inauguration day included an open reception at the White House that became so unruly he had to flee. The public celebrating his victory practically vandalized the Executive Mansion.

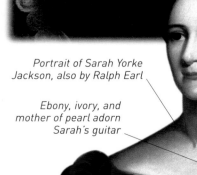

Portrait of Sarah Yorke Jackson, also by Ralph Earl

Ebony, ivory, and mother of pearl adorn Sarah's guitar

Hannah Van Buren

Hannah Hoes and Martin Van Buren were cousins who grew up together in Kinderhook, New York. Hannah died of tuberculosis at age thirty-five.

★

Hannah Hoes Van Buren

PRESIDENT
Martin Van Buren

YEARS AS FIRST LADY
Never served as first lady

BORN
March 8, 1783
Kinderhook, New York

DIED
Age 35
February 5, 1819
Albany, New York

A gentle woman
The Van Burens' 12-year marriage was likely a happy one. A niece said Hannah had a "loving, gentle disposition."

An elegant hostess
Martin's daughter-in-law, Angelica, wore costly jewelry like this as Van Buren's official hostess.

Double strand of pearls

The widower
The widower president moved into the White House with his four grown sons.

Dolley's match
Dolley Madison brought together the Van Burens' son, Abraham, and Angelica Singleton.

Anna Harrison

Anna was the wife of one president and the grandmother of another. She married William Harrison in 1795, and they had 10 children. William held many political offices before becoming president in 1840. Due to the sudden death of their son, Anna could not attend her husband's inauguration. One month later, William Harrison died of pneumonia.

★

Anna Symmes Harrison

PRESIDENT
William Henry Harrison

YEARS AS FIRST LADY
March 4–April 4, 1841

BORN
July 25, 1775
Morristown, New Jersey

DIED
Age 88
February 25, 1864
North Bend, Ohio

A brief first lady
Anna was still packing to travel from Ohio to Washington, D.C., when she learned of her husband's untimely death.

War hero
Harrison defeated Chief Tecumseh at the Battle of Tippecanoe in 1811.

Log cabin campaign
The symbol of the log cabin was used during Harrison's run for the presidency in 1840 to identify William with the common man. This campaign item is from that election.

Letitia Tyler

A little-known first lady
As is the case with so many women of the 19th century, little is recorded about Letitia Christian's early life.

Letitia married John Tyler, a Virginia state legislator, and they then had nine children. A stroke left her partially paralyzed in 1839. John became vice president in 1841. Due to President Harrison's sudden death, however, John became president. After another stroke during John's presidential term, Letitia died in the White House.

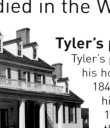

Tyler campaign banner

His Accidency
When William Henry Harrison died in office, Tyler became the first vice president to assume the presidency without being elected. This led his critics to nickname him "His Accidency."

Tyler's plantation home
Tyler's plantation was his home from 1842—the year his wife died—to 1862. It survived the Civil War and is still in the family.

Julia Tyler

After Letitia's death, John soon remarried. The second Mrs. Tyler was a vivacious 24-year-old. She met, and married, Tyler when she moved to Washington, D.C. She spent only a few months as first lady, but delved into her role with enthusiasm.

An enterprising bride
Julia Tyler adored her role as first lady and held frequent dinner parties and receptions. After leaving the White House, she signed some of her letters "Mrs. Ex-President Tyler."

The Rose of Long Island
Julia modeled once in school and later for this advertisement. She called herself the Rose of Long Island.

A pro-slavery president
Tyler supported slavery. His wife did as well, and suffered for it during the Civil War.

Portrait of Sarah Polk painted in 1846, by G. P. A. Healy

Sarah Polk

Sarah was more independent than was acceptable for women of her era. She was educated and preferred politics to music and needlepoint. As first lady, she became known— and sometimes criticized—for her opinions. Childless and with few domestic responsibilities, she became James's adviser in private, read over his speeches, and worked with him on many aspects of state business.

Strict Sarah
Mrs. Polk's strict religious principles led her to prohibit Sunday receptions and dancing at the White House. Still, she proved to be a charming hostess and influential first lady.

Banner from 1844 campaign

POLK AND DALLAS.

Tea at the White House
This elegant teapot, which was probably used by the Polks at the White House, was part of a set purchased for 85 dollars.

Polk for president
Despite lacking charisma, James became the Democratic candidate in 1844, defeating the more personable Henry Clay.

George Washington   *Andrew Jackson*

Martin Van Buren

William Henry Harrison

John Tyler

John Quincy Adams

James Monroe

James Madison

James Polk

Thomas Jefferson

The Polk partnership
James Polk pledged to expand the land held by the US to the Pacific Ocean. He reached his goal with the support of the first lady, who served unofficially as his personal adviser.

John Adams

Sarah's presidential fan
James gave Sarah this fan in 1845 to carry at his inauguration.

Mrs. Zach. Taylor.

Margaret Taylor

★
Margaret Smith Taylor

PRESIDENT
Zachary Taylor

YEARS AS FIRST LADY
1849–1850

BORN
September 21, 1788
Calvert County, Maryland

DIED
Age 63
August 18, 1852
Pascagoula, Mississippi

Refined lady
Mrs. Taylor, who used this calling card and purse, was refined, but cartoonists showed her as a rough frontier woman.

Beaded purse

Margaret spent 15 years moving with Taylor to military posts around the US. She became seriously ill, and though she recovered, she was seen as a semi-invalid. The Mexican War made her husband a general and a hero. After Taylor became president, Peggy asked her daughter Betty to serve as official hostess.

Perfect bliss
There is still debate about whether any authentic images of Margaret Taylor have survived. Her daughter Betty Bliss, pictured here, was only 23 when she took on the duties of running the White House. A lieutenant colonel's wife, Betty had great poise and charm.

Old Rough and Ready
Zach Taylor was a professional soldier and got the nickname "Old Rough and Ready" from the men he commanded. He had no political experience, but won the presidency due to his status as a war hero.

Abigail Fillmore

Abigail was the first of first ladies to have a job before her marriage: she was a teacher for more than six years. As was customary, she gave up her career after she married, but Abigail still made a lasting contribution to future first families by creating a library in the White House.

★
Abigail Powers Fillmore

PRESIDENT
Millard Fillmore

YEARS AS FIRST LADY
1850–1853

BORN
March 13, 1798
Stillwater, New York

DIED
Age 55
March 30, 1853
Washington, D.C.

A great mind
Abigail was highly educated, with a thorough knowledge of the issues affecting her husband's administration.

A hardworking chief executive
Fillmore worked in a textile mill before entering politics. His political success was due to hard work and a supportive wife.

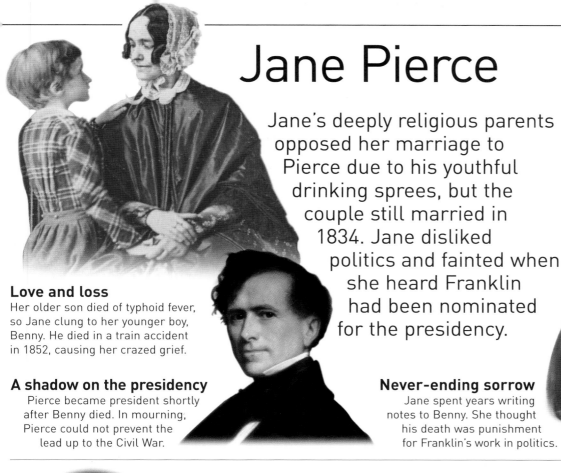

Jane Pierce

Jane's deeply religious parents opposed her marriage to Pierce due to his youthful drinking sprees, but the couple still married in 1834. Jane disliked politics and fainted when she heard Franklin had been nominated for the presidency.

★

Jane Means Appleton Pierce

PRESIDENT
Franklin Pierce

YEARS AS FIRST LADY
1853–1857

BORN
March 12, 1806
Hampton, New Hampshire

DIED
Age 57
December 2, 1863
Andover, Massachusetts

Locket with Benny's photo

Love and loss
Her older son died of typhoid fever, so Jane clung to her younger boy, Benny. He died in a train accident in 1852, causing her crazed grief.

A shadow on the presidency
Pierce became president shortly after Benny died. In mourning, Pierce could not prevent the lead up to the Civil War.

Never-ending sorrow
Jane spent years writing notes to Benny. She thought his death was punishment for Franklin's work in politics.

Harriet Lane

When the bachelor senator James Buchanan became president in 1857, his niece Harriet served as his official hostess. She brought glamour at a time of hostility between the North and South over the issue of slavery. After the Civil War, she married Henry Elliot Johnston, a wealthy banker.

A bachelor's beauty
Harriet was a flirtatious young woman with violet eyes.

★

Harriet Lane

PRESIDENT
James Buchanan

YEARS AS FIRST LADY
1857–1861

BORN
May 9, 1830
Mercersburg, Pennsylvania

DIED
Age 73
July 3, 1903
Rhode Island

Prince of Wales

Harriet Lane

Fit for a prince
In 1860, England's Prince of Wales made a historic visit with President Buchanan and Harriet Lane to Mount Vernon. Miss Lane invited the royal visitor to many White House receptions.

Doomed presidency
The first bachelor to be president, Buchanan was a dignified statesman. Still, he could not avoid blame for the Union's collapse.

Mary Lincoln

Mary Lincoln entered the White House during the Civil War. Well-meaning and intelligent, her southern roots made northerners think she was a spy and southerners see her as a Union sympathizer. Devoted to Lincoln and her position, she left public life briefly when her 11-year-old son, Willie, died in 1862. After Lincoln's assassination in 1865, she was again plunged into grief, from which she never fully recovered.

The first lady's excessive spending on clothes and redecorating of the White House were her attempts to uphold the power and prestige of the presidency during its most serious national crisis

Opposites attract
In many ways, Abe and Mary were opposites. He was extremely tall and thin; she was short and plump. He had grown up in a log cabin in the woods of Kentucky; she had lived a comfortable life in the city. Despite their differences, their mutual interest in politics drew them together.

Schooled on the frontier
Mary's name appears inside Thomas Buchanan Read's *Female Poets in America* (above). Mary was seen as an ignorant frontier girl because she was from Kentucky. But she had received an exceptional education and could discuss anything—from poetry to politics—with the elite members of the nation's capital.

The first family

Mary and Abe had four sons. However, only two, Robert and Thomas, lived past childhood. Eddie and Willie died young. Their loss took its emotional toll on Mrs. Lincoln, who became increasingly odd and unpredictable.

Black stripes

Off-white silk taffeta material

Purple flowers

Game boards

Cards

Spinner

Chess pieces

Dice shaker

Dominoes

Checkers pieces

Dice

Fashion at any cost

In 1861, Mrs. Lincoln wore this two-piece gown (above) for a photograph session with renowned photographer Mathew Brady. The first lady often shopped for fine fabrics in New York and employed a full-time dressmaker, former slave Elizabeth Keckley, who became her close friend.

Growing up in the White House

Thomas "Tad" Lincoln was a boy when his father became president. His game set here shows boards and playing pieces. Tad was only 12 years old when his father died. His mother leaned on him for emotional support as if he were an adult.

Abraham Lincoln

Andrew Johnson

Julia Grant

Ulysses Grant

Mary Lincoln

William Sherman

Lincoln's last reception

On the night of his second inauguration, President Lincoln held a special reception for the heroes of the Union cause. The guests included Major General Ulysses S. Grant and his wife, Julia, Vice President Andrew Johnson, and Major General William T. Sherman. This was the last formal event hosted by the first family. Lincoln was assassinated several weeks later.

Women and the War Between the States

Although President Lincoln believed that "a house divided cannot stand," he could not prevent the southern states from leaving the Union and forming the Confederate States of America. Civil war broke out shortly after his inauguration in 1861. Over the next four years, 600,000 American men lost their lives. Women's lives were dramatically affected by the conflict as well. With their husbands off to war, both northern and southern women took over tasks outside the home. Many nursed the sick and wounded; others raised money for hospitals and military supplies while managing farms or plantations. Mary Lincoln frequently visited the suffering, including African Americans. She was the first woman to invite black people to the White House as guests.

Women with soldier

Harriet Tubman was a runaway slave. Slave owners offered a $40,000 reward for her capture, but she was never caught and the bounty money remained unclaimed

A strong union
Throughout the war, Mary Lincoln supported her husband's political career. The success of the Union army bolstered the Lincoln-Johnson ticket during the presidential campaign of 1864. Lincoln was inaugurated for his second term on March 4, 1865. On April 9, 1865, Robert E. Lee, commander of the Confederate forces, surrendered to Union major general Ulysses S. Grant.

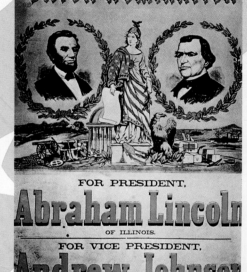

UNION NOMINATION
FOR PRESIDENT,
Abraham Lincoln
OF ILLINOIS.
FOR VICE PRESIDENT,
Andrew Johnson

Poster from 1864 campaign

An elegant protest
Josiah Wedgwood was a famous Englishman who opposed slavery. To further the abolitionist cause, he made a ceramic image of a kneeling slave (below). Cast as a token, the image was distributed by antislavery groups.

United in a common cause
Mary Lincoln supported the abolitionist, or antislavery, movement. Many women who joined abolitionist groups realized they had something in common with those in bondage. They too were denied many basic rights, such as the right to vote. Harriet Tubman, pictured here, personally led hundreds of people to freedom on the Underground Railroad, the name given to a network of secret escape routes that took slaves north.

Bronze metal

AM I NOT A WOMAN & A SISTER 1838

For the ages

On April 14, 1865, Abraham Lincoln was attending the play *Our American Cousin* at Ford's Theater in Washington, D.C., when actor John Wilkes Booth approached Lincoln and shot him in the back of the head. The president was carried across the street to a boardinghouse. There he lay unconscious, surrounded by his family, doctor, and cabinet members. He died the next morning. Following his death, a weeping secretary of war, Edwin M. Stanton, declared, "Now he belongs to the ages."

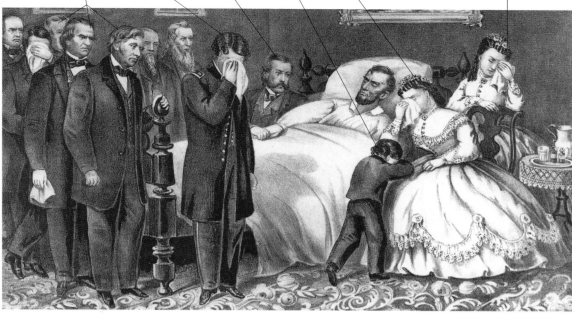

Members of Lincoln's cabinet

Robert Lincoln

Surgeon general

Tad Lincoln

Mary Lincoln

Actress Clara Harris was at the play with the Lincolns

Buildings draped in black funeral bunting

Elaborate funeral car with Lincoln's casket inside

Sixteen gray horses adorned with ostrich plumes

A nation mourns
Tens of thousands of mourners lined the route of Abraham Lincoln's funeral cortege to pay their last respects to the slain president.

Martyred president

After so many losses during the Civil War, the newly reunited nation lost its leader just five days after the official end of the war. Abraham Lincoln's assassination left the country in shock, and Mary was so grief-stricken that she was unable to leave the White House to attend her husband's funeral.

Mary Lincoln in mourning clothes

A symbol of sorrow
In Lincoln's time, the ritual of mourning was quite elaborate, and often lasted for years. After the death of a loved one, women wore special clothes and jewelry, and other items such as this lapel watch (above), to symbolize loss.

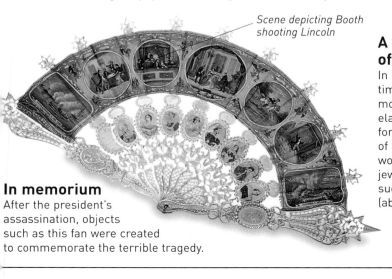

Scene depicting Booth shooting Lincoln

In memorium
After the president's assassination, objects such as this fan were created to commemorate the terrible tragedy.

Eliza Johnson

Eliza rarely left her room in the White House due to her poor health. Still, she contributed greatly to her husband's career, teaching Andrew to read and write in the early years of their marriage, and later raising their five children in Tennessee. When Johnson became president after Lincoln's assassination, Eliza joined him in Washington. However, she was unhappy as first lady, so their daughter Martha acted as hostess for her father.

A hard life
The daughter of a poor shoemaker, Eliza McCardle attended school until her teens, but was then obliged to work.

Ticket to Johnson's impeachment trial

U.S. SENATE
Impeachment of the President
ADMIT THE BEARER
APRIL 17TH 1868.
GALLERY.
Geo. F. Brown
Sergeant-at-Arms

An impeached president
After Lincoln's death, Johnson found himself in control of the Union. In 1868, Congress tried to remove him from office because he opposed their harsh policies toward the defeated South. He was spared by one vote.

Martha was the wife of a senator from Tennessee

White House substitute
Martha Johnson Patterson filled in as hostess for her ill mother, Eliza. Mrs. Patterson was an unassuming woman who remained gracious toward visitors even during her father's impeachment trial.

Julia Grant

Born in rural Missouri, Julia Dent preferred fishing and horseback riding to books. Such spirit appealed to Lieutenant Ulysses S. Grant. After a four-year engagement, during which Grant distinguished himself as a hero in the Mexican War, the two married and had four children. The life of a military wife was difficult, and the couple were apart for long periods. During the Civil War, Grant became leader of the Union army—his victory then enabled the couple to enter the White House on a wave of popularity.

Jubilant Julia
The first lady was delighted to be associated with the capital's rich and famous figures. The sophisticated elite found her direct manner refreshing.

A war hero candidate
After leaving the military in 1854, Grant started businesses, but all failed. The war gave him the chance to try the military again. His success as a presidential candidate was due to his fame as a Union general.

GRANT & WILSON.

Banner from 1868 campaign

A lively family
This portrait shows Nelly and Jesse, the Grants' two youngest children. The lively Grant children were loved by the public.

Julia Dent Grant

PRESIDENT
Ulysses S. Grant

YEARS AS FIRST LADY
1869–1877

BORN
January 26, 1826
St. Louis, Missouri

MARRIED
August 22, 1848
St. Louis, Missouri

CHILDREN
Frederick Dent
Ulysses Simpson
Ellen Wrenshall
Jesse Root

DIED
Age 76
December 14, 1902
Washington, D.C.

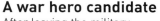

Julia

Ulysses

A sure bet
Julia supposedly went into a silver mine in Nevada after her husband bet she would be afraid to go.

Lucy Hayes

Lucy Hayes was the first college graduate to hold the position of first lady. She was also a woman of strong religious and moral beliefs. A supporter of the Temperance movement against alcohol and drugs, Lucy, with the support of her husband, refused to serve liquor in the mansion. Her ban won her critics and fans. It also earned her the memorable nickname "Lemonade Lucy." Mrs. Hayes declined to act as spokesperson for women's rights groups, who had hoped the educated first lady would become their ally.

Lemonade Lucy

The Woman's Christian Temperance Union commissioned this portrait to honor Lucy Hayes. Although she did not belong to the organization, the first lady's refusal to serve liquor at the White House made her a symbol for women reformers.

Lucy favored simple, dignified dresses rather than high fashion

A fine match

Before Lucy Webb ever laid eyes on Rutherford Hayes, she had heard a lot about him. Their mothers, both widows and church friends, conspired to bring the two together. It was a good match. Rutherford, a popular and honest president, was also a devoted husband and father.

Lucy Webb's diploma from Wesleyan Female College

The "new woman"

Lucy attended Wesleyan Female College in Ohio. At that time, a college-educated girl was seen as a "new woman." Still, Lucy had only two career paths: being a wife and a mother, which she happily accepted.

All-American china
Lucy, a popular hostess, promoted national unity after the war by choosing American themes, such as this native turkey (below), for her official White House china.

Menu and seating plan from a Hayes dinner party

Celebrating the nation's birthday
Exhibitions, such as the one advertised above, celebrated the country's 100th birthday. While the first couple had a strict routine of morning prayers and evening hymn singing, they asked Americans to participate in the various festivities.

The china was designed by Theodore Davis

Modern conveniences
Life in the White House became easier with the arrival of modern conveniences such as this typewriter. A telephone and a permanent running-water system also arrived during the Hayes administration.

Hatchet

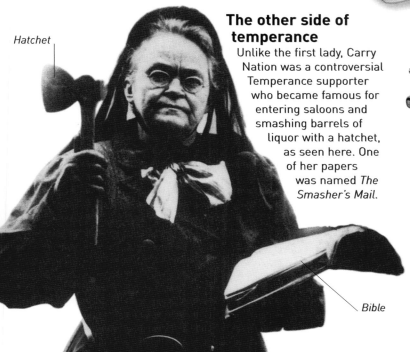

The other side of temperance
Unlike the first lady, Carry Nation was a controversial Temperance supporter who became famous for entering saloons and smashing barrels of liquor with a hatchet, as seen here. One of her papers was named *The Smasher's Mail.*

Bible

Lucretia Garfield

Raised on a farm, Lucretia met James at school. There were long separations from each other during the early years of their marriage when James served as an Ohio state senator, and later when he served in the Civil War. Shortly after James became president, she contracted malaria. While recuperating, Lucretia was shocked to learn that James had been shot.

Creative lady

Lucretia's diaries show a wise and creative woman who acted as an adviser to James. Sadly, she was to preside over a president's funeral.

Banner from 1880 campaign

From poverty to politics

James Garfield, portrayed on this presidential campaign banner, rose from poverty to become a lawyer, Civil War hero, preacher, and successful politician. His wife kept him from falling prey to scandal and corruption, which had ruined many aspiring politicians of that time. His term in office was cut short by an assassin's bullet.

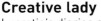

Satin train

Charles Guiteau

President Garfield

Lucretia in satin

The first lady wore this gown to the 1881 inaugural ball at what is now the Smithsonian's Arts and Industries Building. The *Washington Post* noted that "Mrs. Garfield's toilet [costume] was a reception dress of delicately shaded lavender satin."

Lace trim

A fatal shot

On July 2, 1881, Charles Guiteau, angered that he could not obtain a federal job, shot the president. A bullet entered Garfield's back and the wound became infected. Lucretia nursed James for more than two months, but he eventually died.

Ellen Arthur

Just as Chester Arthur's political career was taking off, his wife, Ellen, died of pneumonia. Ellen met Chester Arthur when he was a young lawyer. He later became a Union general in the Civil War. After he became president in 1881, Arthur's sister Mary McElroy served as his official hostess.

Ellen, known as Nell
Ellen Arthur was a fashionable young woman and an accomplished singer. She died suddenly in January 1880—eight months before her husband became president.

Arthur was an elegant dresser

Mending his ways
Seen as a dishonest politician, Arthur might not have become president, had it not been for Garfield's assassination. In the White House, he changed his ways and started the Civil Service Commission, hiring workers based on skills, not connections.

Uncontrolled growth
During Arthur's presidency, the country's population grew enormously, with new immigrants arriving daily. Leaving poor conditions in their native lands, passengers on ships such as this one faced uncertain destinies in their new home. The rapid influx of foreigners to the cities strained services and raised tensions among ethnic groups.

Mary Arthur McElroy was Chester Arthur's youngest sister

Official hostess
Mary Arthur McElroy served as official hostess during much of her brother's presidency. Chester, however, pined for Nell and never truly allowed anyone to take her place. He often organized official social events himself.

Frances Cleveland

Frances Folsom was a 21-year-old beauty, and Grover Cleveland was a 48-year-old bachelor. They married in the White House—a first for a president. Frances's picture soon appeared in newspapers, magazines, and advertisements. As first lady, she became an icon. Some historians think that her popularity helped Cleveland—the only president to serve two nonconsecutive terms—return to the White House. The notoriety did not stop there. The Clevelands' first baby, Ruth, had her own fans, and a candy bar was named in her honor.

The picture of beauty

The stunning Frances Folsom became a celebrity when she married portly Grover Cleveland on June 2, 1886. However, because Frances thought it was improper for women to speak out in public, she was never interviewed about her marriage.

Ivory satin

India muslin

Exquisite simplicity

The day after Frances's wedding to Grover Cleveland, the *Washington Post* wrote a glowing report of her wedding gown, calling it "an enchanting white dress of ivory satin."

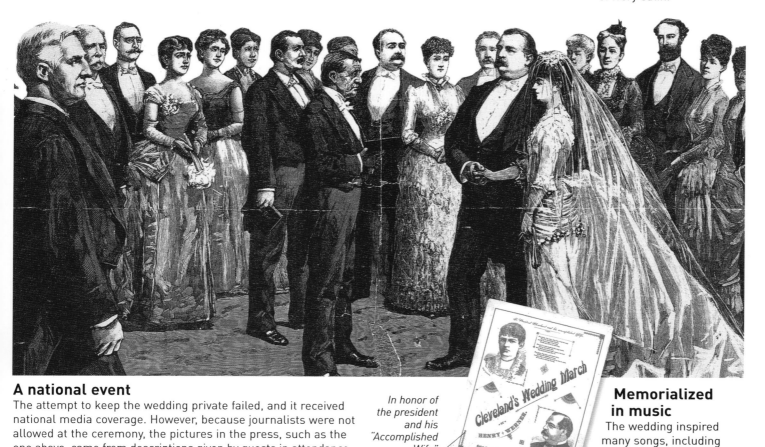

A national event

The attempt to keep the wedding private failed, and it received national media coverage. However, because journalists were not allowed at the ceremony, the pictures in the press, such as the one above, came from descriptions given by guests in attendance.

In honor of the president and his "Accomplished Wife"

Cleveland's Wedding March

HENRY WEBER

Memorialized in music

The wedding inspired many songs, including this wedding march (left).

Defeat and victory

Cleveland was the only president to serve two nonconsecutive terms. After winning the election of 1884—the election from which this campaign banner (left) comes—he lost in 1888, then made a comeback in 1892.

Grover's 1884 campaign was haunted by a scandal: that he had fathered an illegitimate child

To date, Frances Cleveland is the youngest first lady

Winning votes

When Cleveland ran again in 1888, the Democrats recognized his wife's popularity and used her image on plates, buttons, and posters. Pictured on this plate (above) without the president, the first lady won support of her own.

Frances Folsom Cleveland

PRESIDENT
Grover Cleveland

YEARS AS FIRST LADY
1886–1889
1893–1897

BORN
July 21, 1864
Buffalo, New York

MARRIED
June 2, 1886
White House, Washington, D.C.

CHILDREN
Ruth
Esther
Marion
Richard Folsom
Francis Grover

DIED
Age 83
October 29, 1947
Baltimore, Maryland

Queen of diamonds

Frances Cleveland

Grover Cleveland

Frances's image appeared everywhere, even on unlikely objects such as playing cards (right). While her popularity helped her husband politically, the president became incensed by the threat to his family's privacy. He tried to stop Frances's likeness from being used in advertising through the passage of a new law, but failed.

The first lady was seen as a symbol of domestic happiness

Thread forms heart shape

A natural-born hostess

At his bride's first White House reception, Grover had been so pleased with her social grace that he playfully announced to her mother, "She'll do!" Frances's popularity increased due to the Saturday receptions she hosted for working women, who could not visit the White House during the week.

An advertising gimmick

This ad (above), shows the first couple bound in a heart of thread, to suggest that marital love keeps the country united. It also reveals how shamelessly advertisers used Frances to sell products.

Caroline Harrison

While Benjamin started his political career, Caroline distinguished herself as a volunteer for the sick and orphaned. As first lady, Caroline advanced worthy causes. She was the first president general of the Daughters of the American Revolution and became a fund-raiser for the Johns Hopkins University Medical School—after they agreed to accept female students. She died in the White House in 1892, leaving her daughter to act as official hostess.

Creative Carrie
A White House visitor recalled that Mrs. Harrison, nicknamed "Carrie," applied her skills in music, art, and design to create an atmosphere of "genteel gaiety."

Goldenrod pattern

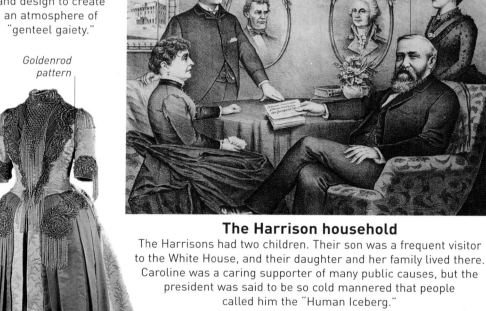

Caroline   Russell   Benjamin   Mary

Top of her class
Mrs. Harrison's father, who spent most of his career as a mathematics professor, believed in providing a good education for his daughters. In 1849, he established the Oxford Female Institute in southern Ohio, from which Carrie, a fine student, received this diploma (above).

The Harrison household
The Harrisons had two children. Their son was a frequent visitor to the White House, and their daughter and her family lived there. Caroline was a caring supporter of many public causes, but the president was said to be so cold mannered that people called him the "Human Iceberg."

Brocaded fabric, woven in New York

A goldenrod gown
Mary wore this gown (above) to the inaugural ball. Her father's favorite flower is woven into the fabric.

A house fit for a first family
This photo from inside the White House was taken about the time of its modernization.

⭐

Caroline Scott Harrison

PRESIDENT
Benjamin Harrison

YEARS AS FIRST LADY
1889–1892

BORN
October 1, 1832
Oxford, Ohio

MARRIED
October 20, 1853
Oxford, Ohio

CHILDREN
Russell Benjamin
Mary Scott

DIED
Age 60
October 25, 1892
Washington, D.C.

Ida McKinley

Ida Mckinley was both beautiful and educated. She attended private schools and learned about business from her father, a wealthy banker. However, Ida's life took a tragic turn after her marriage to William. The deaths of her mother and then, months later, her infant daughter caused a nervous breakdown, followed by epileptic seizures. Strangely, after her husband was shot in 1901, Ida's seizures disappeared.

A sense of style
Ida's affliction made social events a burden, but she refused to delegate her duties to an official hostess. The first lady owned a wardrobe of elegant gowns and fashionable accessories, such as this fan (left), to keep up appearances for White House visitors.

A difficult wife
As first lady, she was demanding throughout her illness, but her husband remained devoted to her.

Mother of pearl

Silk fabric

Badge of support
This badge (left), worn by voters during McKinley's 1896 campaign, proved that a political wife could have influence. Ida did all she could to advance William's career.

Pink and blue flowers

Preference for flowers
During her time as first lady, Mrs. McKinley used several different sets of china, many of which had floral designs. These plates (right) are made of English porcelain.

McKINLEY THE IMMORTAL.

"It is God's Way"

SONG With Refrain

BY EMMA MAGRUDER

DEDICATED TO THE DEVOTED WIFE OF OUR MARTYRED PRESIDENT

PUBLISHED BY THE MARCLAY MUSIC CO. 335 Shawmut Avenue, BOSTON.

Memorial music
In 1901, the president was assassinated by an anarchist. Memorial works such as this song (above) were composed in his honor.

Edith Roosevelt

Edith Carow and Teddy Roosevelt were childhood playmates, but it was not until he was a widower with a daughter that they married. After he became president in 1900, Edith managed the restoration of the White House—adding the West Wing and a picture gallery of first ladies. With six unruly children, Edith also hired the first social secretary to help control her family's image.

Rough Rider
In the Spanish-American War, Theodore created a volunteer cavalry regiment known as the "Rough Riders." Their victorious charge up Cuba's San Juan Hill led to a Spanish surrender and earned Roosevelt hero status.

Calm in the storm
Edith stayed calm among the havoc in the White House. Whether her sons were leading their pony through the corridors or sliding down the staircase, she was still in control.

Painted wood

Moose on wheels
Although Roosevelt hunted big game, his grandchildren contented themselves with this pull-toy.

Edith Roosevelt's name stamped on the flap

★

Edith Kermit Carow Roosevelt

PRESIDENT
Theodore Roosevelt

YEARS AS FIRST LADY
1901–1909

BORN
August 6, 1861
Norwich, Connecticut

MARRIED
December 2, 1886
London, England

CHILDREN
Alice Lee (stepdaughter)
Theodore
Kermit
Ethel Carow
Archibald Bulloch
Quentin

DIED
Age 87
September 30, 1948
Oyster Bay, New York

Princess Alice
The only person Edith could not control was Alice, her rebellious stepdaughter. Known as Princess Alice, the headstrong girl dared to smoke in public.

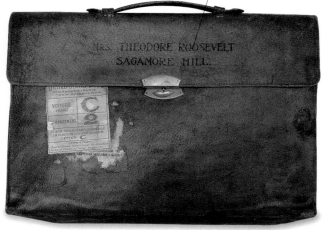

MRS. THEODORE ROOSEVELT
SAGAMORE HILL

A world traveler
The first lady carried this leather attaché case on trips to Panama, Europe, and Brazil with the president.

Helen Taft

An independent young woman, Helen formed her own salon, or intellectual group, at the age of 22 and invited young attorney William Taft to join. The two married years later. Just two months into Taft's presidency, Helen suffered a stroke. She still managed, however, to put her own stamp on the White House.

Ambitious Helen
Helen had more enthusiasm for her husband's post as US governor to the Philippines than he did. She hoped it would lead him to the presidency.

Breaking traditions
Helen played an important role in Will's career. Perhaps that is why the first lady broke with tradition on inauguration day by riding with her husband to the White House, instead of behind in a separate vehicle.

William

Helen

Fur trim

Fleece lining

Goldfish and lotus designs

Chinese robe
Helen's Manchu-style coat (left) was meant to be worn in cold weather. While living in the Philippines, Mrs. Taft made a trip to China to escape the tropical heat, and may have purchased the coat there.

Signs of the times
As the nation changed from a farming culture to an industrialized one, the Tafts' cow was the last one to graze on the White House lawn. The Tafts also bought the first White House automobile.

A lovely legacy
Helen had the thousands of Japanese cherry trees that bloom each spring planted in the capital.

Ellen Wilson

Ellen Wilson was an accomplished painter, a lover of literature, and a mother of three. When Woodrow started his political career, she helped him edit and rehearse speeches and advised him on issues. Ellen wanted to improve conditions in the nation's cities. She supported a bill in Congress on slum clearance. Called the Ellen Wilson Bill, it passed in 1914, shortly before her death from an incurable kidney ailment.

Ellen Axon Wilson

PRESIDENT
Woodrow Wilson

YEARS AS FIRST LADY
1913–1914

BORN
May 15, 1860
Savannah, Georgia

MARRIED
June 24, 1885
Savannah, Georgia

CHILDREN
Margaret Woodrow
Jessie Woodrow
Eleanor Randolph

DIED
Age 54
August 6, 1914
Washington, D.C.

A perfect partner

Ellen Wilson is largely credited for her husband's success. She proved to be the perfect partner for a man who needed the support and encouragement of a devoted wife.

US Capitol

Win with Wilson

Ellen wholeheartedly supported Woodrow's rise in politics. She was delighted with his presidential win in 1912, the election from which this campaign pennant (left) comes. Wilson was a man of strong ideals, whose struggle to prevent American involvement in World War I failed. The United States eventually entered the conflict in 1917.

Wilson campaign pennant

Margaret
Jessie
Eleanor
Ellen
Woodrow

The Wilsons at home

Woodrow Wilson was a popular professor at Princeton University before entering politics. This photograph of their three daughters (above) was taken in 1911, after Wilson became governor of New Jersey.

The Ellen Wilson Bill

This photograph shows an alley dwelling in Washington, D.C., in 1908. Shocked by these deplorable living conditions, the first lady became an advocate for housing reform.

Edith Wilson

Edith had no formal schooling until her teenage years, but she went on to become one of America's most influential first ladies. She was first married to Norman Galt, who died suddenly and left her a wealthy widow. Years later, she met, and then married, the recently widowed Woodrow Wilson. When the president suffered a paralyzing stroke in 1918, Edith was accused of running the government single-handedly.

★

Edith Bolling Galt Wilson

PRESIDENT
Woodrow Wilson

YEARS AS FIRST LADY
1915–1921

BORN
October 15, 1872
Wytheville, Virginia

MARRIED
December 18, 1915
Washington, D.C.

DIED
Age 89
December 28, 1961
Washington, D.C.

The gatekeeper
Edith screened her husband's visitors and mail. The press often criticized her influence on the presidency.

Mrs. Wilson at home
"At home" cards, such as this one for Mrs. Wilson (left), announced the days and times when a first lady wished to receive visitors at the White House.

Mrs. Wilson
At Home
Friday afternoon
May 23d
from five until seven o'clock

Initials standing for Young Women's Christian Association

Gifts of peace
This pin and box were presented to Mrs. Wilson by the people of Paris in 1919, when she traveled with Woodrow to France for the peace negotiations after the end of World War I.

Diamonds

Lalique glass doves

FOR EVERY FIGHTER
A WOMAN WORKER
Y.W.C.A.
BACK OUR SECOND LINE OF DEFENSE
UNITED WAR WORK CAMPAIGN

Lalique glass box

The second line of defense
Women played a critical role in the war effort, as this World War I poster shows. This included the first lady. She decoded diplomatic and military messages sent from Europe to the president.

Mrs. Wilson and the Nineteenth Amendment

Although the US is a democracy, women were not allowed to vote until 1920. Women began to fight for this basic right in the mid-1800s. The suffrage—or right-to-vote—movement was led by feminists such as Lucretia Mott and Susan B. Anthony. In the early 1900s, they picketed, lobbied, marched, and petitioned Congress. Despite being one of the nation's most powerful first ladies, Edith Wilson opposed the suffrage movement. Even so, the Nineteenth Amendment, by which women won the right to vote, was passed during Wilson's administration.

Suffrage sash over armor

RESPECTFULLY INSCRIBED TO THE SUFFRAGISTS OF THE W

MARCHING ON TO VICTORY

WORDS BY SCHUYLER GREENE

MUSIC BY OTTO MOTZAN

50¢

Marching on to victory

Support for the suffrage movement took many forms. This sheet music (above) shows a suffragist announcing a new day.

A crusader's cape

Suffragists wore this uniform to show solidarity and gain publicity.

The procession drew 5,000–8,000 thousand marchers

Official Program WOMAN SUFFRAGE Procession

VOTES FOR WOMEN

Washington D.C. March 3, 1913

US Capitol

Purple, white, and gold were the colors of the militant wing of the suffrage crusade

Suffrage herald

A march on Washington

Suffragists marched through Washington, D.C., just one day before the Wilsons moved into the White House. Angry spectators attacked and spat on many marchers—requiring the US Cavalry to restore order.

White House gate

Button of the National Woman Suffrage Association

VOTES FOR WOMEN

Button of the National Woman Suffrage Association

Button of a pro-suffrage women's club

HOUSEWIVES LEAGUE

The pro faction

Men were needed to support suffrage as well; without their votes, the Nineteenth Amendment could not pass. Men and women ran a nationwide political campaign to win public approval, producing buttons, banners, and other materials to further their cause.

MR. PRESIDENT HOW LONG MUST WOMEN WAIT FOR LIBERTY

Freedom for their daughters

This scrapbook (above) belonged to the Men's League for Woman Suffrage—one of the first pro-suffrage groups started by men. Similar groups appeared across the country.

WOMEN HAVE NO RIGHT TO VOTE

Anti-suffrage buttons

The losing side

The "antis" who were against the Nineteenth Amendment lost when it was finally added to the US Constitution on August 26, 1920.

How long must women wait?

In January 1917, a group of radical suffragists picketed in front of the White House. Though infuriated, Mrs. Wilson asked them to come in from the cold. They refused her invitation and were later sent to jail for picketing and disturbing the peace.

ANTI SUFFRAGE

Florence Harding

Florence was strong and self-reliant. She first married at 19, but her husband was an alcoholic and abandoned her and their son. Years later, she met and married Warren Harding, a newspaper editor. He used his newspaper to make political connections while Florence ran the circulation department. Later, she took credit for managing his presidential campaign. A government corruption scandal marked her time in the White House, which was cut short by Warren's death in 1923.

Hard times for Harding
The likable Warren Harding chose advisers poorly, and as a result, his administration was weakened by charges of scandal and corruption.

A suffrage supporter
Supporting suffrage, Florence played an important role in the first election in which women voted in 1920. Some Harding supporters received this badge (left).

The duchess
A woman who was both admired and ridiculed for her folksy midwestern style, Mrs. Harding was called the "Duchess" by her husband and his friends.

Flapper style
Florence Harding's flapper-style dress, which she wore to the 1921 inauguration ceremony, was at the height of fashion during the 1920s.

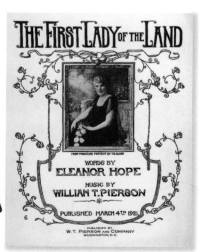

The first lady of the land
This sheet music (above) from 1921 honors the new first lady. Mrs. Harding served as her husband's unofficial campaign manager, and once said, "I know what's best for the president. I put him in the White House."

Pearlized sequins over delicate tulle

Florence Kling Harding

PRESIDENT
Warren G. Harding

YEARS AS FIRST LADY
1921–1923

BORN
August 15, 1860
Marion, Ohio

MARRIED
July 8, 1891
Marion, Ohio

CHILDREN FROM FORMER MARRIAGE
Marshall deWolfe

DIED
Age 64
November 21, 1924
Marion, Ohio

Grace Coolidge

Unlike her husband, who was nicknamed Silent Cal, Grace Coolidge was sociable. She taught at the Clarke School for the Deaf in Massachusetts, where she met and married Calvin, a lawyer. Warren Harding's death in 1923 catapulted Coolidge to the presidency and Grace into the public eye. Her years in the White House were marred by the death of her son, Calvin Jr., yet Grace still managed to shine as first lady.

An animal lover
During her years as first lady, Mrs. Coolidge populated the White House with many unusual pets, including this raccoon named Rebecca.

Silent Cal
Calvin Coolidge was an honest man who rarely smiled and seldom spoke. Grace liked to tell this story about her unusually quiet husband: A Washington hostess once bet Coolidge that she could make him say more than two words. The president replied, "You lose."

Grace Coolidge dress from the 1920s

An occasional extravagance
Though normally frugal, Coolidge did buy his wife stylish clothing (left) to set off her good looks.

Turquoise

Silver

Jewelry with a special meaning
The first lady wore this silver-and-turquoise bracelet of Native American design (above). Calvin had Indian ancestors and considered his membership in the Sioux tribe a great honor.

An advocate for the deaf
Helen Keller, who was both deaf and blind, came to the White House in 1926. In order to "hear" the first lady, Keller placed one hand on Mrs. Coolidge's neck and held the other one to her lips.

Lou Hoover

Lou was the first woman to earn a degree in geology from Stanford University. After graduation, she married Herbert Hoover. His business took them to posts around the world. During World War I and throughout the Great Depression, which began in 1929, Lou devoted herself to public service. In the White House, she supported women's and civil rights, while maintaining her role as first lady.

The driver is made of painted cast iron

The lighter side of Lou
Generally a quiet companion to her husband in public, Lou sometimes did show a sense of humor to the public.

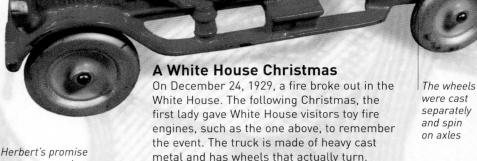

A White House Christmas
On December 24, 1929, a fire broke out in the White House. The following Christmas, the first lady gave White House visitors toy fire engines, such as the one above, to remember the event. The truck is made of heavy cast metal and has wheels that actually turn.

The wheels were cast separately and spin on axles

Herbert's promise to speed up recovery did not work with voters

A self-made man
Herbert Hoover was an American success story. He grew up an orphan and became a millionaire. During World War I, Herbert served as an effective administrator of humanitarian aid to Europe.

SPEED UP RECOVERY
RE-ELECT
HOOVER
KEEP HIM ON THE JOB

The Great Depression
On October 24, 1929, the New York Stock Market crashed, starting the Great Depression. Many people lost their jobs, as well as their life savings, and President Hoover was often blamed. Although he tried to boost the nation's hopes for recovery, Herbert lost his bid for reelection in 1932.

The Girl Scout's Promise

On my Honor I will try

To do my Duty to God and my Country

To help other People at all times

To Obey the Scout Laws

Season's Greetings

Christmas card from the Hoovers

Scout's honor

An advocate for active and self-reliant women, Lou Hoover was a supporter of the Girl Scouts and promoted the organization by inviting troops to the White House. She had a long-term commitment to the group, having been sworn in as a troop leader in 1917. In 1922, Lou was elected national president and, as first lady, became the Girl Scouts' honorary national president. Mrs. Hoover's involvement with the group enabled her to offer progressive views about women's self-esteem and leadership abilities without appearing too political.

126,515,000 Girl Scouts stamps were issued

Stamp of approval

This stamp (below) was issued on July 24, 1962, to promote the Girl Scouts of America.

PRESIDENT'S WIFE STRESSES VITAL PART SCOUTING PLAYS IN LIFE OF TODAY'S GIRLHOOD

Speaking up for girls

During her term as first lady, Mrs. Hoover was a distinguished guest at the National Girl Scouts Convention. She frequently spoke to girls of the value of social service and volunteerism, two lifelong commitments of her own.

On the air

On March 24, 1931, the first lady addressed the nation's Girl Scouts by radio, thanking them on behalf of herself and the president for their outstanding efforts to help the needy. Lou was the first presidential wife to use radio to promote her views.

★ Lou Henry Hoover

PRESIDENT
Herbert Hoover

YEARS AS FIRST LADY
1929–1933

BORN
March 29, 1874
Waterloo, Iowa

MARRIED
February 10, 1899
Monterey, California

CHILDREN
Herbert Clark
Allan Henry

DIED
Age 69
January 7, 1944
New York, New York

Eleanor Roosevelt

Raised by her grandmother after losing her parents, Eleanor married her fifth cousin, Franklin. After having six children, one of whom died in infancy, she devoted her life to politics, helping Franklin's career after he contracted polio. During the Great Depression, Eleanor brought hope to millions of suffering Americans.

A "useful" first lady

Eleanor went from being a solemn child to being an ambitious first lady who said in her early days at the White House, "There may be ways in which I can be useful."

Eleanor, already a Roosevelt, did not have to change her name after marriage

Franklin

Eleanor

James

Anna

The Roosevelt family

The Roosevelts—who were distant cousins as well as husband and wife—are seen here with their two oldest children.

FDR

Franklin Roosevelt, or FDR, was the only president to serve three terms in office. Despite his crippling polio, he was able to perform his tasks as president, mostly due to the efforts of his amazing wife.

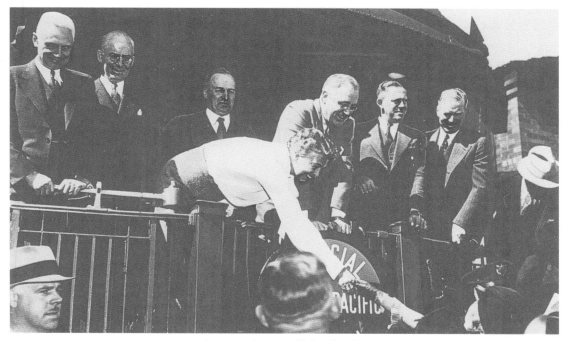

A popular political wife
A good campaigner, Eleanor accompanied her husband on campaigns, pausing to shake hands with supporters. She did this to help Franklin, whose illness made him tire easily.

Anna Eleanor Roosevelt

PRESIDENT
Franklin D. Roosevelt

YEARS AS FIRST LADY
1933–1945

BORN
October 11, 1884
New York, New York

MARRIED
March 17, 1905
New York, New York

CHILDREN
Anna Eleanor
James
Elliott
Franklin Delano
John Aspinwall
One boy who died in infancy

DIED
Age 78
November 7, 1962
New York, New York

Eleanor's initials appear on the clasp

This belt is a reproduction

Clothes befitting a first lady
Eleanor wore this velvet day dress (right) to her husband's first inauguration on March 4, 1933. This shade of lavender is called Eleanor blue. After her White House years, Mrs. Roosevelt donned this mink coat (above) on special occasions. It has a gold clasp inscribed with her initials.

A nation's hunger
In this photograph from 1932 (left), Eleanor serves food to the needy at a soup kitchen in New York City.

President Franklin Roosevelt

The New Deal
The New Deal, promoted in this music (above), was a program created to help people find work after the Depression.

A wartime ambassador

Eleanor used her great communication skills to calm the fears of the public and boost morale during World War II. Following America's entry into the war in 1941, she traveled around the world to visit US troops. In 1942, she became the only first lady to fly by herself across the Atlantic. While in Europe, she toured the bombed areas of London, visited women's training centers, and inspected American Red Cross units. By acting as unofficial ambassador for the president, she made a great contribution to the nation's war effort.

A bearer of goodwill
Mrs. R., as Eleanor was often called, extended her influence beyond the home front during World War II. Her presence abroad gave US forces hope and kept up their spirits. Here, she visits troops stationed in Central America.

This poster quotes FDR

"We are now in this war"
Quoting from a speech by President Roosevelt, this poster (above) served to boost morale among Americans, whose husbands, fathers, sons, and brothers were leaving home for the uncertainty of war.

The first lady as social activist

Called the First Lady of the World by President Harry S. Truman, Eleanor Roosevelt was one of the greatest humanitarians of the 20th century. As first lady, she worked tirelessly to improve the lives of the underprivileged. After being widowed at age 60, she continued to serve her country as the US delegate to the United Nations. Eleanor was also a firm advocate of civil rights, and fought to end segregation and discrimination. Remembered for her great compassion, Mrs. Roosevelt remains one of the most respected first ladies.

Eleanor on her wedding day

Eleanor as a child

Eleanor as a young woman

Eleanor in later life

Honoring a special woman
This quilt (above), sewn by Callie Fanning Smith in 1940, was made to honor the first lady. It is composed of cloth squares featuring portraits of Eleanor Roosevelt and scenes from her life.

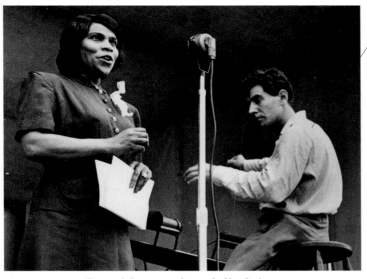

Conductor and pianist Leonard Bernstein

Speaking up for civil rights

In 1939, Marian Anderson, a famous singer, was not allowed to perform at Constitution Hall in Washington because she was African American. The first lady helped arrange a concert for Marian on the steps of the Lincoln Memorial instead.

A way with words

Eleanor used this desk when writing. During the Depression, she wrote a column that appeared in hundreds of newspapers. She also wrote a best-selling book about her early life.

133,170,000 stamps were issued

A declaration of human rights

Harry Truman, Franklin's successor as president, gave Eleanor a post with the United Nations. She led the creation of the U.N.'s Universal Declaration of Human Rights, stating the basic principles of human rights in the modern world. Eleanor worked at the U.N. until she was almost 70 years old.

ELEANOR ROOSEVELT
5¢ U.S. POSTAGE

A model American

One of many acts honoring Eleanor was this five-cent stamp, issued in her memory in 1963.

THE UNIVERSAL DECLARATION OF **Human Rights**

The declaration was adopted in 1948

Bess Truman

After leaving the White House, Truman declared that his wife had been his "chief adviser" and "full partner." Indeed, Bess had always worked alongside her husband. When he became vice president, Bess became a paid staff member in Harry's office. After Roosevelt's death, Truman became president, and Bess faced the predicament of unwanted fame.

A private first lady
Mrs. Truman, who disliked social functions and held no press conferences, was respected as a no-nonsense woman and loyal wife.

Badge from 1948 campaign

"The buck stops here"
Truman coined this phrase. It symbolized his devotion to the office and how seriously he took his presidential responsibilities. One of his most difficult duties was to bring about the end of World War II with the decision to drop atomic bombs on two Japanese cities.

The boss's dress
Mrs. Truman, whose husband called her the Boss, wore this dress (left) to the inaugural reception on January 20, 1949. It was designed by Polo Gowns of Paris and New York.

Pearl gray damask with gold thread

Whistle-stop campaigning
Bess generally shied away from the media attention brought by Truman's reelection campaign. This is a rare photo of her campaigning with her husband.

Presidential seal

Presidential china
The Trumans purchased a set of china for the White House. The plates have a green border edged in gold.

50

Mamie Eisenhower

Years of experience in handling challenging social situations helped Mamie when her husband, Dwight D. Eisenhower, the former supreme allied commander of US forces in Europe during World War II, became president. Her loving and wealthy father was concerned that his daughter would not be happy as a soldier's wife, but Mamie lived up to the task.

A distinctive first lady
Mamie Eisenhower put her personal stamp on the White House. The first lady tried to make the White House a cozy home for her husband and herself.

A charmed life
The 34 charms on Mamie's bracelet represent meaningful events in Ike's life.

West Point insignia

Four-leaf clover for luck

Jeep with "Ike" on hood

PI for Philippine Island service

Likable Ike
Dwight, nicknamed Ike, was an optimistic man who was openly affectionate toward his wife. Americans were fond of him.

★

Mamie Doud Eisenhower

PRESIDENT
Dwight D. Eisenhower

YEARS AS FIRST LADY
1953–1961

BORN
November 14, 1896
Boone, Iowa

MARRIED
July 1, 1916
Denver, Colorado

CHILDREN
Doud Dwight
John Sheldon

DIED
Age 82
November 11, 1979
Gettysburg, Pennsylvania

They liked Ike's wife!
A devoted wife, mother, and hostess, Mamie appealed to housewives, who felt they had something in common with the most visible woman in the country. She became a celebrity in her own right. Mamie tackled her role with enthusiasm, running the White House with precision while charming the nation.

A political pig
The Santa Barbara Republican Women's Organization sold this piggy bank (left) as a fund-raising item in 1956.

MAMIE Prosperity

Mamie's personalized cooler

1952 Republican National Convention Chicago Illinois — MRS. 'IKE' EISENHOWER

MAMIE PAT

Popular with the public
As this button (left) shows, Mamie Eisenhower and Pat Nixon—the wives of the presidential and vice presidential candidates of 1952 and 1956—were popular. They were very appealing to women, who were voting in equal numbers with men.

Jacqueline Kennedy

The glamorous Jacqueline Kennedy, or Jackie, was a symbol of elegance in the 1960s. Young, wealthy, intelligent, and beautiful, she grew up on an estate on Long Island and in a Park Avenue townhouse in New York City. While working as a photographer for the *Washington Times-Herald,* Jackie met a witty and handsome young congressman from Massachusetts named John F. Kennedy. Their storybook wedding in 1953 drew thousands of reporters and onlookers.

Jack Bouvier

Jackie Bouvier

John Bouvier

The Jackie look
Jackie was always known for style. As first lady, her fashion sense influenced public taste and inspired a new look.

A childhood passion
Jackie's father, Jack Bouvier, was a wealthy stockbroker, and her mother was a talented equestrienne. Taking after her mother, Jackie won two national riding competitions by age seven. Her other childhood passion came from her grandfather, John Bouvier, who inspired her to read and write poetry.

On assignment

With this bulky camera on hand (below), Jackie pursued interesting stories throughout the capital. She interviewed truck drivers and congressmen, laborers and actresses.

Jacqueline Bouvier Kennedy

PRESIDENT
John F. Kennedy

YEARS AS FIRST LADY
1961–1963

BORN
July 28, 1929
Southampton, New York

MARRIED
September 12, 1953
Newport, Rhode Island

CHILDREN
Caroline Bouvier
John Fitzgerald
Patrick Bouvier

DIED
Age 64
May 19, 1994
New York, New York

The inquiring camera girl

After winning a *Vogue* writing contest, Jackie thought of becoming a journalist. In late 1951, she was offered a position with the *Washington Times-Herald*, and became the paper's "Inquiring Camera Girl" in 1952.

Jackie's Graflex camera

Ivory silk wedding gown with portrait neckline

2.88-carat diamond

2.84-carat emerald

An extraordinary engagement

While at the newspaper, Jackie met the man she later called "the choicest bachelor in the Senate." John F. Kennedy, called Jack, was the son of a millionaire, a Harvard University graduate, and a World War II hero.

The fairy tale begins

In 1953, 24-year-old Jacqueline married the 36-year-old senator, John Kennedy. Thousands of reporters and spectators jostled for position outside the church for a glimpse of the newlyweds. After the ceremony, there was an outdoor reception at Hammersmith Farm. More than 1,200 guests—members of high society as well as politicians—attended.

A youthful White House

Although in private their marriage was not always happy, Jack and Jackie used the media to promote an image of contentment to the public. Often photographed with their two children, the Kennedys appeared to be the model American family. Jackie soon proved that she was ambitious in the White House. As the first lady, she used her knowledge of art to oversee a restoration project that changed the White House into a national showcase.

Kennedy ribbon

John, Jr.

Jackie

Caroline

Jack

A new voice

In a famous speech, Kennedy said, "Ask not what your country can do for you, ask what you can do for your country."

The first family

Mrs. Kennedy was delighted with the birth of Caroline in 1957 and John Jr. in 1960. She once told an interviewer, "If you bungle raising your children nothing else much matters in life." She was determined to shelter her son and daughter from the attention directed at them by their father's position. However, commercial products, such as this comic book, did appear with their likenesses.

Caroline Kennedy

Gray brocade jacket

A-line dress

Setting trends

Jackie wore this suit in 1961. Women were so taken with her fashion style that department stores used mannequins with her features and hairstyle.

After Camelot

President Kennedy was assassinated in Dallas, Texas, on November 22, 1963. The press compared the end of the Kennedy administration to the end of Camelot, the mythical kingdom of King Arthur. Within hours of her husband's death, Jackie bravely stood by Vice President Lyndon Johnson as he took the oath of office and became president. Later, she directed many of the funeral details with remarkable dignity. The stunned country shared her grief.

In homage
This medal (above), with the portrait of John F. Kennedy, was designed by noted American artist Paul Manship.

A solemn oath
Vice President Lyndon Johnson was sworn in as president shortly after Kennedy's death. The ceremony took place on *Air Force One*, the president's plane. Dazed but dignified, Jackie stood by Johnson's side, still wearing her suit stained with Jack's blood.

Robert F. Kennedy

Jean Kennedy Smith

Peter Lawford

Jacqueline Kennedy

Caroline Kennedy

John F. Kennedy Jr.

Grief and strength
Millions of viewers worldwide watched the president's state funeral. Most were in awe of Jackie's strength as she led her young children down the steps of the US Capitol after the service. Not since the assassination of Abraham Lincoln nearly one hundred years earlier had there been such an outpouring of national grief.

Jackie O.
At 40, Jackie shocked the nation by marrying Greek shipping magnate Aristotle Onassis. After his death in 1975, Jackie O., as she was called, became a respected book editor.

John F. Kennedy Jr.

Caroline Kennedy Schlossberg

Mrs. Onassis

President Clinton

Leaving a legacy
Jackie established the John Fitzgerald Kennedy Library to commemorate Jack's life. Here, the family speaks with President Bill Clinton at the library in 1993.

Lady Bird Johnson

Claudia, or Lady Bird, Taylor lost her mother when she was just five. Lady Bird worked hard for each of her husband's campaigns for congress and vice president. When Johnson was sworn in as president after Kennedy's assassination in 1963, she was at his side.

Claudia Taylor Johnson

PRESIDENT
Lyndon B. Johnson

YEARS AS FIRST LADY
1963–1969

BORN
December 12, 1912, Karnack, Texas

MARRIED
November 17, 1934
San Antonio, Texas

CHILDREN
Lynda Bird, Luci Baines

DIED
Age 94, July 11, 2007
West Lake Hills, Texas

Beautifying America
Lady Bird created an awareness of the environment and promoted programs to improve conditions in poverty-stricken neighborhoods.

Model of Lady Bird's campaign train

Campaign button

Conductor's hat with *Lady Bird Special* patch

Lady Bird's train
During the 1964 presidential campaign, the first lady made a solo, four-day train trip through the South. From Virginia to Louisiana, she promoted Lyndon's reelection and talked about his political plans.

Turbulent presidency
Lyndon's presidency saw more protests against the Vietnam War. He decided eventually to drop his reelection campaign and retire to their Texas ranch.

America's mineral heritage
Presented to Lady Bird in 1967, this pin (right) represents America's gem and mineral wealth. There are 100 stones, from all 50 states, as well as the District of Columbia.

American eagle made of gold

A head start in life
Mrs. Johnson supported Head Start, a program designed to teach learning skills to low income children, giving them a "head start" in life. Lady Bird also advised her husband on political issues.

Pat Nixon

Pat Nixon lost both parents by age 18 and worked through college during the Great Depression. Although she disliked politics, she campaigned for her husband. When Richard Nixon won the presidency in 1968, Pat became a goodwill ambassador, traveling around the world on diplomatic missions. Like some of the first ladies before her, Mrs. Nixon became a target during a turbulent period in US history, with protests against the president's policies on civil rights, women's rights, and the war in Vietnam.

The faithful first lady
Pat shared in her husband's victories and defeats. Here, they attend their daughter's wedding in 1971.

Pat paid official visits to 82 nations during her term as first lady

Great Wall of China

A historic event
The Nixons made a historic visit to China in 1972. Their trip to China helped expand trade and cultural exchanges between the two countries.

vietnam moratorium

No more war!
Nixon's presidency was plagued by the Vietnam War, which had not been resolved during Johnson's term. While US soldiers died, protests increased at home. The dove of peace, featured in this button (left), became a symbol for the antiwar movement.

Nixon was the only president to resign from office, and was later pardoned of any wrongdoing by his successor

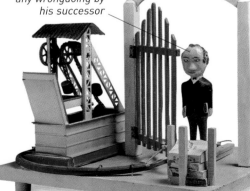

WATER GATE

A president's downfall
Nixon was charged with covering up a break-in at the Democratic Party offices in Washington's Watergate complex and resigned. Above is a folk artist's representation of the scandal.

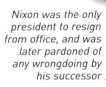

Thelma Catherine Ryan Nixon

PRESIDENT
Richard M. Nixon

YEARS AS FIRST LADY
1969–1974

BORN
March 16, 1912
Ely, Nevada

MARRIED
June 21, 1940
Riverside, California

CHILDREN
Patricia
Julie

DIED
Age 81
June 22, 1993
Park Ridge, New Jersey

Betty Ford

Betty was not afraid to speak about her personal life. Becoming first lady after Nixon's resignation, she walked into her first news conference and declared her support of the arts, the elderly, and the Equal Rights Amendment (ERA)—feminist legislation opposed by her husband. The first lady's openness about her breast cancer, and later, problems with painkillers and alcohol, inspired many to talk openly about their own issues. After Ford left office, Betty got professional help for her addictions, urging others to do the same. Later, she founded the Betty Ford Center for Drug and Alcohol Rehabilitation.

Ready for Betty
One of Betty's aides called her "the most up-front person I ever knew." Some Americans disliked Betty's outspokenness, but most were ready for a first lady who said, "being ladylike does not require silence."

Elizabeth Bloomer Ford

PRESIDENT
Gerald R. Ford

YEARS AS FIRST LADY
1974–1977

BORN
April 8, 1918, Chicago, Illinois

MARRIED
October 15, 1948
Grand Rapids, Michigan

CHILDREN
Michael Gerald, John Gardiner, Steven Meigs, Susan Elizabeth

DIED
Age 93, July 8, 2011
Rancho Mirage, California

First Mama vest worn by Betty

Gerald Ford became president without having been elected by the public, the only chief executive to do this

"10-4 First Mama"
Betty was given the affectionate handle "First Mama" by CB (citizens band) radio users. The public was not so fond of Gerry.

WASHINGTON STATE WOMEN'S POLITICAL CAUCUS
BETTY, YES! GERRY, NO.
1505 - 10th AVE. EAST, SEATTLE, WA. 98102

Button from 1976 campaign

An unelected president
After Nixon's, and then his vice president, Spiro Agnew's, resignation, Gerry Ford was appointed as president and tried to restore Americans' confidence in the presidency.

Autographs of the Washington Redskins players

First down, Betty
Gerry was a star on a college football team. After breast cancer surgery, she received this ball from an NFL team.

GAME BALL
AWARDED TO
MRS. BETTY FORD
FROM COACH GEORGE ALLEN
AND WASHINGTON REDSKINS
WASHINGTON 30 - DENVER 3
SEPTEMBER 30th, 1974
MONDAY NIGHT FOOTBALL

Rosalynn Carter

Rosalynn Smith was 18 when she married US Navy midshipman Jimmy Carter. Traveling to six naval bases in seven years opened up an exciting world for Rosalynn. When Jimmy was elected governor of Georgia, she entered the world of politics. As first lady, Mrs. Carter combined southern charm with a remarkable strength of will. Some reporters called her "Steel Magnolia."

Expanding the first lady's role

Mrs. Carter attended cabinet meetings and commissions. Jimmy asked her to represent him on an official trip to Latin America, where she discussed policies with foreign leaders. She was criticized for exceeding the limits of her position.

Jeweled purse

King Hassan II of Morocco gave this beautiful purse to the first lady.

Jimmy Carter

Adviser and activist

Rosalynn, seen here with her husband in the Oval Office, was a trusted adviser. In her first year as first lady, she traveled widely in the US and abroad, held many press conferences, and hosted dozens of receptions.

Equal Rights Amendment

Mrs. Carter stands with Betty Ford (right) at an ERA rally. She shared Betty's support of an amendment to the Constitution giving equal rights to all, regardless of sex.

The hostages were released in January 1981

The hostage crisis

In 1979, militant Iranians took over the US embassy in Tehran and held 66 Americans hostage. Followers of the Ayatollah Khomeini, they opposed US policies against their leader. Carter failed to release the hostages, hurting his presidency. The hostages were finally released on Carter's last day in office.

Rosalynn Smith Carter

PRESIDENT
Jimmy Carter

YEARS AS FIRST LADY
1977–1981

BORN
August 18, 1927
Plains, Georgia

MARRIED
July 7, 1946
Plains, Georgia

CHILDREN
John William
James Earl III
Jeffrey
Amy Lynn

Nancy Reagan

Nancy Reagan was fiercely protective of her husband and often faulted for having too much power over affairs of state. Nancy grew up in Chicago and later became a Hollywood actress. After marrying actor Ronald Reagan in 1952, she raised their two children while he started his political career. After entering the White House, Nancy was criticized for her expensive spending habits. Later, she changed her image to reflect her social concerns.

Just Say No

Mrs. Reagan adopted drug abuse as her cause and traveled throughout the nation, making appearances to encourage children to "Just Say No" to drugs.

⭐

Nancy Davis Reagan

PRESIDENT
Ronald Reagan

YEARS AS FIRST LADY
1981–1989

BORN
July 6, 1921, New York, New York

MARRIED
March 4, 1952
San Fernando Valley, California

CHILDREN
Patti Davis, Ronald Prescott

DIED
Age 94, March 6, 2016
Los Angeles, California

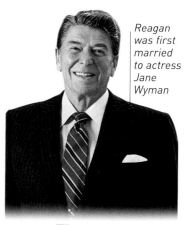

Reagan was first married to actress Jane Wyman

The great communicator

A former actor and an extremely popular president, Ronald Reagan was noted for his ease in front of TV cameras.

Inaugural elegance

The first lady's 1981 inaugural gown (left) is made of white lace over silk satin and embroidered with beads. It was designed by James Gallanos.

China scandal

Nancy's purchase of a new set of White House china for $200,000—in fact a private gift—was criticized due to cuts to programs for the poor by Reagan.

Caricature of Ronald Reagan

Voodoo economics

This voodoo doll (right) may be a reference to Reagan's "voodoo economics" policies.

Barbara Bush

Barbara Bush devoted her White House years to the cause of literacy. She avoided the controversies that plagued many former first ladies by staying silent about political issues that would interfere with her husband's policies, and focusing instead on humanitarian concerns. George and Barbara met as teenagers and married during World War II. Mrs. Bush has written books to support reading programs nationwide as well as a best-selling autobiography.

A life of service
Bush was a congressman, UN ambassador, director of the CIA, and VP. Barbara's charm was a great asset to his career.

Barbara and Millie
First dog Millie (above) became a celebrity when Barbara wrote *Millie's Book*, a springer spaniel's view of the White House.

Dan Quayle was Bush's running mate in 1988 and 1992

Stories to grow on
Mrs. Bush often visited schools, where she read to children. She organized the Barbara Bush Foundation for Family Literacy—yet still found time to read to her grandchildren.

No second chance
A strong leader in foreign affairs, Bush was less successful at grappling with economics and crime. Voters did not reelect him in 1992.

★

Barbara Pierce Bush

PRESIDENT
George H. W. Bush

YEARS AS FIRST LADY
1989–1993

BORN
June 8, 1925
Bronx, New York

MARRIED
January 6, 1945
Rye, New York

CHILDREN
George Walker
Robin
John Ellis
Neil Mallon
Marvin Pierce
Dorothy

General Norman Schwarzkopf, commander of US forces

George Bush

Barbara Bush

First lady in the field
In 1991, President Bush sent US troops to the Middle East to defend Kuwait, a small nation with valuable oil resources, from its Iraqi invaders. When George visited American soldiers in the war zone, the first lady accompanied him.

Hillary Clinton

Hillary spent much of her time as first lady leading a task force on US health-care reform. After Bill left office, she served two terms as a US senator. In 2008, she made an unsucessful bid for the White House, losing the primary race to Barack Obama. From 2009 to 2013, she served as Obama's secretary of state. In 2016, she was the Democratic candidate for president but lost the election.

A political partner

Hillary helped Bill reach his political ambitions, but she was hurt in 1998, when he admitted to having a relationship with an intern.

Bill Clinton

Taking office

On January 20, 1993, the day Bill Clinton was sworn in as president, the Clintons marched down Pennsylvania Avenue in the inaugural parade and then moved into the White House with their daughter, Chelsea.

Senator Edward Kennedy of Massachusetts, esteemed legislator

The senator

Hillary served two terms as senator for New York, working effectively with Democrats and Republicans in Congress. She served on the Budget, Armed Services, Health, and Education committees, and obtained funding to help her state after the terrorist attacks of September 11, 2001.

Topping the ticket

After a hard contest with Bernie Sanders for the Democratic nomination, Hillary became the first woman in the country's history to top the presidential ticket of a major political party. She was not successful in her run for the presidency.

★

Hillary Rodham Clinton

PRESIDENT
William Jefferson Clinton

YEARS AS FIRST LADY
1993–2001

BORN
October 26, 1947
Park Ridge, Illinois

MARRIED
October 11, 1975
Fayetteville, Arkansas

CHILDREN
Chelsea

Laura Bush

As an only child, Laura Welch had a sheltered upbringing in Texas. Prior to marrying George W. Bush, she was a teacher and earned a degree in library science. Although Laura was never an outspoken political partner, she left her mark on many education and literacy projects during the six years her husband was governor of Texas. As first lady, she continued to focus on education and family issues.

A good match
Together, Laura and George weathered the controversial election of 2000, as well as the tragic events of September 11, 2001.

"I never felt I was so traditional. . . . I felt I was in many ways very contemporary."

Laura Bush: Traditional First Lady With a Twist

Making headlines
Although Laura Bush was first lady of Texas, the national press was just getting to know her during her husband's run for the presidency. This *New York Times* headline (above) tried to put her life into perspective for voters.

Button from 2000 campaign

America's Next First Family

George & Laura Bush

Running for first lady
Campaign buttons for Bush (left) featured Laura. Her image as a teacher, librarian, wife, and mother helped their cause.

★

Laura Welch Bush

PRESIDENT
George W. Bush

YEARS AS FIRST LADY
2001–2009

BORN
November 4, 1946
Midland, Texas

MARRIED
November 5, 1977
Midland, Texas

CHILDREN
Barbara
Jenna

Laura Bush campaign button

A family tradition
Laura and her mother-in-law, Barbara, both first ladies, shared an interest in education and literacy. Barbara's husband and son both became president.

Michelle Obama

Michelle Obama attended Princeton University and earned a law degree from Harvard. While working at a Chicago law firm, she met and married Barack Obama, who shared many of her ideals. Michelle balanced career and family, serving in community-focused positions and raising her daughters. As the first African-American first lady, she devoted herself to positive social change, with a focus on childhood obesity.

Top priority
The Obamas' two daughters, Malia and Sasha, have always been Michelle's top priority. They were the first young children to live in the White House since Jimmy Carter's daughter, Amy.

Speaking her mind
A dynamic speaker, Michelle first caught the public's attention at the 2004 Democratic National Convention. She spoke at rallies, gave interviews, and attended conferences during Barack's campaigns for president.

What's in a bump?
When Barack Obama won the Democratic nomination in 2008, Michelle congratulated him with a fist bump. The friendly gesture caused a media frenzy.

The campaign trail
Although reluctant to take time away from her career, Michelle scaled back her duties at work to focus on her husband's campaign. For over a year, she traveled around the US, listening to voters' concerns and spreading her husband's message of hope and change.

Michelle Robinson Obama

PRESIDENT
Barack Obama

YEARS AS FIRST LADY
2009–2017

BORN
January 17, 1964
Chicago, Illinois

MARRIED
October 3, 1992
Chicago, Illinois

CHILDREN
Malia
Sasha

Melania Trump

PRESIDENT
Donald Trump

YEARS AS FIRST LADY
2017–

BORN
April 26, 1970
Novo Mesto, Slovenia (part
of the former Yugoslavia)

MARRIED
January 22, 2005
Palm Beach, Florida

CHILDREN
Barron

Melania Trump

Melania Trump was born Melanija Knavs (Germanized to Melania) in Slovenia, then part of communist Yugoslavia. Her father worked as a car dealer and her mother was a seamstress. She entered the University of Ljubljana, but left to pursue a modeling career. She became an American citizen in 2006. She is the first first lady born outside of the US since Louisa Adams, wife of John Quincy Adams.

Ivanka
Trump, Donald's
eldest daughter

Melania

Trump family campaigns

Donald Trump, surrounded by family, delivers a speech at the South Carolina primary. His family took an active role in his campaign. Daughter Ivanka was particularly prominent at rallies and in interviews. While Melania was not comfortable in the limelight, Ivanka was at ease in front of the camera. Ivanka assumed many campaign functions typically performed by a presidential candidate's spouse.

Family first

Melania is a devoted mother to Barron, the youngest of Donald's five children. Donald Trump has four adult children from his previous two marriages: Donald Jr., Ivanka, Eric, and Tiffany. Melania is also involved in national and international charities that benefit children.

Convention speech

Melania delivered a rare and somewhat controversial speech at the Republican National Convention. The press noted that it echoed many of the words from Michelle Obama's speech at the 2008 Democratic National Convention.

Trump 2016

Trump's campaign to "Make America Great Again" focused on reforming immigration and refugee policies, reducing taxes, increasing US military might, and fighting terrorism.

Did you know?

FASCINATING FACTS

Abigail Adams

Jacqueline Kennedy's Emmy Award

★ Abigail Adams asked her husband to "remember the ladies" when he was helping to write the nation's Declaration of Independence in 1776.

★ Dolley Madison is the only first lady to receive an honorary seat on the floor of Congress.

★ Elizabeth Monroe ended the custom in which a president's wife made the first social call on the wives of other officials in Washington. The insulted women boycotted her White House receptions.

★ Eliza Johnson taught her husband how to spell and pronounce words properly.

★ Julia Grant owned slaves during the Civil War, while her husband served as general of the Union Army. After the war, the family employed paid African-American servants.

★ Ida McKinley once worked as a bank teller and manager.

★ Ellen Wilson, Woodrow Wilson's first wife, was the only professional artist to serve as first lady.

★ Lou Hoover graduated from Stanford University with a geology degree.

Painting by Ellen Wilson

★ Bess Truman worked as her husband's salaried aide during his time in the Senate.

★ Jacqueline Kennedy won an Emmy Award for her television tour of the White House in 1962.

★ Lady Bird Johnson conducted her own campaign for her husband's election. She also lobbied for environmental protection.

★ Pat Nixon worked her way through college in the Great Depression and helped establish the first White House tours for the blind and deaf.

★ Betty Ford once worked as a professional dancer with the Martha Graham Company. She also founded the Betty Ford Center, a nonprofit rehabilitation center for people struggling with drug and alcohol addiction.

Betty Ford at the Betty Ford Center

★ Nancy Reagan worked as a Hollywood actresss in the 1950s. In 1957, she appeared on screen with her husband for the first and only time, in the movie *Hellcats of the Navy*.

Grant family with servant

Movie lobby card

QUESTIONS AND ANSWERS

Q Which first lady was the daughter of a British army officer?

A Elizabeth Monroe's father, Lawrence Kortright, was a wealthy New York merchant. During the American Revolution, he remained loyal to the king and served as a captain in the British Army. In the end, he had most of his fortune confiscated due to his pro-British actions and beliefs.

Q Which first lady interviewed her future husband for a newspaper before he became president?

Jackie's camera

A Jacqueline Bouvier worked as an "inquiring camera girl" for the *Washington Times-Herald* after graduating from George Washington University in 1951. While at the paper, she interviewed Congressman John F. Kennedy. She married him in 1953.

Q Which first ladies were divorcées when they married their husbands?

A Rachel Jackson had a brief marriage before marrying Andrew Jackson. Florence King DeWolfe, a divorcée with one son, married Warren G. Harding in 1891. Elizabeth Ann Bloomer divorced her first husband, William Warren, in 1947. She married Gerald Ford a year later.

China platter featuring a turkey

Q Which first lady chose the most controversial design for the White House china?

A Lucy Hayes. The china's design was the result of a chance meeting between Lucy and artist Theodore R. Davis in 1879. Mr. Davis suggested using the flora and fauna of North America as a theme for the White House tableware. He eventually produced 130 different designs of American plants, animals, and scenic views. He also created unique shapes for the dishes. Although art critics were extremely critical of the new china, the designs were well liked by the American public.

Q Which first lady was the first to have a graduate degree?

A Pat Nixon was the first president's wife to enter the White House with a graduate degree. Following four years of study at the University of Southern California, she graduated with the equivalent of a master's degree and became a teacher. She continued to teach for the first year of her marriage.

Lansdowne Portrait

Q Which first lady saved a famous painting from being destroyed?

A In 1814, the British Army invaded Washington and set fire to the White House. Dolley Madison managed to escape just before the troops arrived. On her way out, she grabbed the famous full-length painting of George Washington known as the "Lansdowne Portrait."

Q How has the role of the first lady changed in the modern age?

A Over the years, the role of first lady has evolved from that of a hostess to encompass humanitarian work and even policy-making. Eleanor Roosevelt broke the mold in the 1930s, when she spoke out for the civil rights of African Americans and the poor.

FIRST LADIES FIRSTS

- Abigail Adams was the first woman whose husband and son were president.
- Dolley Madison was the first American to respond to a telegraph message.
- Julia Tyler was the first wife of a president to be photographed.
- Abigail Fillmore was the first first lady to earn a salary before marriage.
- Frances Cleveland was the first wife of a president to marry and give birth in the White House.
- Florence Harding was the first wife of a president able to vote for her husband.
- Grace Coolidge was the first wife of a president to speak in sound newsreels.
- Eleanor Roosevelt (right) was the first first lady to hold press conferences.

- Jacqueline Kennedy was the first wife of a president to hire a press secretary.
- Pat Nixon was the first wife of a president to wear pants in public.
- Michelle Obama was the first African-American first lady.

MARY LINCOLN

Illustrated copy of the Emancipation Proclamation

Mary Lincoln was raised in a household that had slaves. However, she was not a supporter of slavery. She deplored the practise and later became an ardent abolitionist.

During the Civil War, Mary supported the war effort. She worked as a nurse, shared intelligence, and offered her advice to the president on military personnel. Her largest contribution, however, may have been her influence on her husband about the issue of slavery. While Lincoln questioned the wisdom of freeing the slaves, she insisted that emancipation was the only moral path. When the Emancipation Proclamation was issued in 1863, for Mary it was a personal victory.

Mrs. Lincoln supported groups that assisted soldiers and freed slaves. On a personal level, Mary was also accepting of race. Her most sympathetic friend and confidante during her years in the White House was her dressmaker, former slave Elizabeth Keckley.

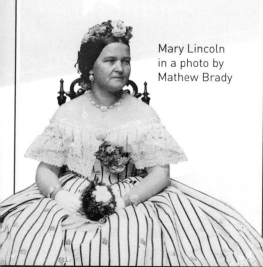

Mary Lincoln in a photo by Mathew Brady

Making a difference

The main role of the earliest first ladies was to serve as the White House hostess. Over time, the role has grown, and first ladies have devoted more energy to worthy causes. The women on these pages stand out as advocates for change.

ELLEN WILSON

Ellen Wilson

Ellen Wilson made many contributions as first lady, but she had the greatest impact on housing reform. Mrs. Wilson toured Washington, D.C., and got a firsthand glimpse of the poor living conditions of the city's slums. She supported the Alley Dwelling Bill, which would destroy the slums and create better housing for Washington's poor. Unfortunately, Mrs. Wilson was also being affected by a kidney ailment at the time. Knowing that she did not have long to live, she begged her husband to support the bill. Just before she died, in 1914, the bill was passed.

Washington, D.C., tenement houses photographed in 1908

FLORENCE HARDING

Florence Harding was one of the early first ladies to push her role beyond that of an official hostess. She wanted to help women understand government, and she invited women's political groups, female federal workers, women in college, and high-school girls to the White House.

At a time when women in the US had just earned the right to vote, Florence promoted the economic, political, and social equality of the sexes. She saw housewives as financial managers and knew what went into raising a family. She

Harding badge for women voters

welcomed divorced women to social events. Having seen her fellow suffragists put in jail, she also became an advocate for prison reform, supporting a bill that would help female inmates learn skills for work. Mrs. Harding expressed her support for all women, saying: "Let women know and appreciate the meaning of being an American—free and equal."

Florence Harding in 1922

ELEANOR ROOSEVELT

Eleanor Roosevelt was a civil rights advocate at a time of segregation. One of her most famous acts in this regard involved the African-American opera singer Marian Anderson. In 1939, Anderson wanted to give a performance at Constitution Hall in Washington, D.C. However, her requests were refused because the hall's owners, the Daughters of the American Revolution, prohibited African Americans from performing there.

Eleanor Roosevelt was a member of the Daughters of the American Revolution. On learning of the situation, the first lady sent a letter to the organization's chairwoman announcing her resignation. This act by the first lady sparked a media frenzy and won public support for Anderson's cause.

In the end, Marian Anderson never did sing at Constitution Hall. Instead, with the help of the Roosevelt administration, she gave an outdoor concert at the base of the Lincoln Memorial. The concert was attended by 75,000 people and broadcast across the country.

Eleanor Roosevelt, shown after her time as first lady

LADY BIRD JOHNSON

Lady Bird Johnson promoted conservation long before the environment was an issue. She had always loved the land and felt its beauty was slipping away. Perhaps the word most closely associated with her years in the White House is "beautification." It covered many of her areas of work—including rural and urban environmentalism, the conservation of national parks, anti-pollution measures, landscaping, and urban renewal.

Many of Lady Bird's efforts focused on Washington, D.C. She created the Committee for a More Beautiful Capital, whose efforts resulted in the planting of thousands of trees, plants, and flowers around Washington's public buildings. She also helped improve the National Mall and created new gardens on the lawn of the White House. She felt that improving the environment in poor neighborhoods also inspired people to help themselves.

NANCY REAGAN

Early on, Nancy Reagan focused on redecorating the living quarters at the White House and holding state receptions. But by 1982, Nancy began to devote herself to an issue that would define her time as first lady—drug abuse.

Mrs. Reagan's focus was on prevention programs for young people. She visited schools and rehabilitation centers, appeared on talk shows, and delivered public service announcements. The motto of her program was: "Just Say No."

When President Reagan signed an anti-drug bill into law in 1986, she appeared with him to discuss the issue. In 1988, Nancy spoke to the General Assembly of the United Nations about the growing international problem of drugs.

Nancy Reagan speaking at an anti-drug rally in 1988

MICHELLE OBAMA

In 2010, Michelle Obama established "Let's Move!" to raise awareness of childhood obesity and encourage children and families to improve their nutritition and physical fitness. Michelle visited schools across the country to spread awareness, and asked government leaders and food manufacturers to produce and serve better school lunches. In 2011, President Obama signed the Healthy, Hunger-Free Kids Act, which funds fitness and nutrition education and gives greater access to free school meals.

Michelle Obama addressing students at a 2013 event

Find out more

Throughout American history, presidential spouses have made great contributions to American life. You can learn more about them in books, museums, and on the internet. As the home to every first lady and gentleman since Abigail Adams, Washington, D.C., is a great place to start. Other sites, such as the First Ladies National Historic Site in Canton, Ohio, also offer a wealth of information.

The Smithsonian
The museums of the Smithsonian Institution have a wealth of exhibits relating to the first ladies. Many of the objects in this book are on display at Washington's National Museum of American History, including everything from official china to inaugural gowns.

The White House
With a reservation, visitors can tour the beautiful White House, where the first ladies have served as hostess. Guests can take part in seasonal events, such as the candlelit Christmas Tour and the famous kids-only Easter Egg Roll.

Potomac parks
In early spring, the famous cherry trees are in full blossom in Washington, D.C. The pink blossoms of more than 3,000 trees cover hundreds of acres of park along the Potomac River and beyond. On the other side of the river, the Lady Bird Johnson Park on Columbia Island makes a beautiful visit, too.

USEFUL WEBSITES

- The National First Ladies' Library site features biographies, timelines, photographs, and a full catalog of first lady resources:
www.firstladies.org

- For facts on White House history, visit The White House Historical Association:
www.whitehousehistory.org

- The White House website contains information on the current first family, as well as a gallery of presidents and first ladies: www.whitehouse.gov

- The Women's History site on About.com presents information on the lives of all kinds of notable women throughout history, including all the first ladies of the United States:
womenshistory.about.com

First Ladies National Historic Site

In 2000, the US government established the first official historic site dedicated to first ladies. Operated by the National First Ladies' Library, the site encompasses the historic family home of Ida McKinley, as well as a museum. Visitors can see exhibits related to first ladies throughout the history of the US.

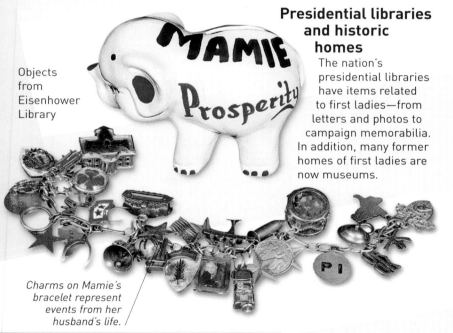

Objects from Eisenhower Library

Charms on Mamie's bracelet represent events from her husband's life.

Presidential libraries and historic homes

The nation's presidential libraries have items related to first ladies—from letters and photos to campaign memorabilia. In addition, many former homes of first ladies are now museums.

First ladies on the screen

Jacqueline Kennedy's TV special, *A Tour of the White House with Mrs. John F. Kennedy,* debuted on February 14, 1962, and is now online at www.hulu.com. During the tour, the charming first lady details the renovations of the White House. You can also see Eleanor Roosevelt on screen: The 1965 Oscar-winning documentary *The Eleanor Roosevelt Story* is now available on DVD.

PLACES TO VISIT

NATIONAL MUSEUM OF AMERICAN HISTORY, WASHINGTON, D.C.
The Smithsonian's National Museum of American History preserves more than three million artifacts, including many objects belonging to US first ladies.

MOUNT VERNON, ALEXANDRIA, VA
Although this was George Washington's home and plantation, Martha took care of the farm when he was away. Visitors can see where Mrs. Washington entertained guests and enjoy the view of the Potomac from the lawn.

RONALD REAGAN PRESIDENTIAL LIBRARY, SIMI VALLEY, CA
This library features many fascinating exhibits, including a painstaking re-creation of the Oval Office, and a permanent exhibit dedicated to Nancy Reagan.

ELEANOR ROOSEVELT NATIONAL HISTORIC SITE, HYDE PARK, NY
In 1927, Eleanor Roosevelt established Val-Kill Industries, a place where local farm families could produce useful products to earn extra income. Today, the site receives visitors year round.

LADY BIRD JOHNSON WILDFLOWER CENTER, AUSTIN, TX
Founded by Lady Bird Johnson in 1982, this botanical garden introduces visitors to the beautiful wildflowers native to Mrs. Johnson's home state.

JOHN F. KENNEDY PRESIDENTIAL LIBRARY, BOSTON, MA
At the JFK Library, visitors can see many items related to Jacqueline Kennedy, including her Emmy Award and one of her famous trendsetting dresses.

MARY TODD LINCOLN HOUSE, LEXINGTON, KY
This two-story brick building was the childhood home of Abraham Lincoln's wife, Mary. In 1977, the house became the first historic site restored in honor of a first lady, and is now home to many historical artifacts.

Index

Acknowledgments

The author and publisher offer their grateful thanks to: Edith P. Mayo, curator emeritus at the Smithsonian's National Museum of American History; Ellen Nanney and Kealy Gordon of the Smithsonian's Office of Product Development and Licensing; Kate Henderson of the Smithsonian's National Museum of American History; Heather Egan and Beverly Cox of the Smithsonian's National Portrait Gallery; Jim Bruns and James O'Donnell of the Smithsonian's National Postal Museum; Robert Johnston of the Smithsonian American Art Museum; the following curators, archivists, and photography professionals from both presidential libraries and private institutions: James Hill, Don Holloway, Mark Renovitch, Michelle Frauenberger, Anthony Guzzi, Mindy Haines, Isabel Parker, Harmony Haskins, Marion Kamm, Maureen Harding, Jennifer Pedersen, Susan Naulty, Debbie Bush, Kathy Tabb, David Stanhope, Victoria Kalemaris, Thomas Price, Kay Tyler, David Smolen, Kelly Fearnow, Allison Enos, Kelly Cobble, Hanna Edwards, Peggy Flynn, and Bettina Demetz; especially Oliver, Nicholas, and Peter Pastan; Dianne Carroll who provided additional photography; and Anna Fischel for proofreading the relaunch version, and Vicky Richards and Antara Raghavan for editorial assistance on it.

PICTURE CREDITS:
(t = top; b = bottom; l = left; r = right; c = center; a = above)

Alamy: 70bl William S. Kuta, 71tl Andre Jenny. Alamy Stock Photo: 62b Jennifer Mack, 65cla Richard Ellis. AP/World Wide Photos: 50lb. Archive Photos: 55lb Express Newspapers, 55br Gary Cameron. Bold Concepts: 63c. George Bush Presidential Library: 61tl, 61lc, 61b. Jimmy Carter Library: 59lc, 59lb, 59rc. Corbis: 7t Todd Gipstein, 47t, 52l, 62ra Ron Sachs/CNP, 63tl, 63b, 66bl Bettmann, 66br David J. & Janice L. Frent Collection, 67br Hulton-Deutsch Collection, 68br Bettmann, 69cla Bettmann, 71bl Bettmann, 71br Farrell Grehan. Chicago Historical Society: 27b. Dorling Kindersley: 64c Kellie Walsh/4eyesphotography.com, 66c (frame), 67cr (frame). George Eastman House: 38b. Dwight D. Eisenhower Library: 51lb, 51rc, 51ra, 71ca, 71cb. Gerald R. Ford Presidential Museum: 58lc, 58rb Dianne Carroll. Getty Images: 64tr, 65cra Debra L Rothenberg / FilmMagic, 65crb Drew Angerer, 65bl Robyn Beck / AFP, 68cr, 69clb Time & Life Pictures, 69br Win McNamee, 70cr. Rutherford B. Hayes Presidential Center: 28rb, 29c. The Hermitage, Home of President Andrew Jackson, Nashville, TN: 16tl, 16c, 16cb, 16r. Herbert Hoover

Library: 44ca, 45tl, 45lb. Andrew Johnson National Historic Site, Greeneville, TN: 26rb. Lyndon B. Johnson Library/Robert Knudsen: 69tr. John F. Kennedy Library: 52r, 53tl, 53ca, 53b, 53r, 54tl, 55tr, 55c, 56tr, 67cl. Library of Congress: 14lc, 17t, 17lb, 18tl, 18cb, 22l, 23b, 25lb, 26l, 30tl, 31tl, 35tl, 37bl, 37br, 38tl, 42l, 43rb, 50tl, 51tl, 68tl, 68cl, 68bl. Mary Todd Lincoln House: 22c. James Madison's Montpelier, Orange, VA: 13lb, 13cb. Monticello/Thomas Jefferson Memorial Foundation, Inc.: 10–11b, 11tl, 11lc, 11c, 11tr. Mount Vernon Ladies' Association: 5rc, 5rb, 6c, 7lb, 7c. National Archives and Records Administration: 47ca. National Museum of American Art, Smithsonian Institution: 5lb, 15t, 16c, 21lc, 21lb, 57c. National Museum of American History: 4c, 5tr, 6tl, 6tr, 9tr, 13rc, 15c, 17ca, 17rb, 18c, 19c, 19rc, 20tl, 20la, 23tl, 23c, 24tr, 25c, 25lb, 26r, 27rc, 30bl, 32b, 32tr, 33tl, 33lb, 33c, 33r, 35c, 37ra, 39la, 42b, 42c, 42cr, 43c, 43ra, 44cb, 45la, 47l, 47c, 50rb, 51rb, 54rb, 60c, 60rb, 62l. National Portrait Gallery: 4l, 5lc, 6b, 7b, 8tr, 10tl, 12b, 13tl, 13rb, 14rc, 15lb, 17ca, 17cb, 18rb, 19lb, 20lc, 20rb, 20ca, 21rb, 22tr, 25tr, 26ca, 27tl, 27tr, 29rc, 31rc, 34c, 38bl, 39tr, 42tr, 43lb, 44lb, 47rb, 48tl Ruth Orkin, 50ca, 51ca, 56ra, 59tl, 60bl, 67cr. National Postal Museum: 45r, 49rc. New Hampshire Historical Society: 20tl, 20rc. New York Times: 56tl George Tames, 63ca. Richard Nixon Library and Birthplace: 57tl, 57lb. Courtesy of Obama for America: 64cl, 64bl. James K. Polk Memorial Association, Columbia, TN: 19tl,

19rb. Ronald Reagan Library: 60tl. Franklin D. Roosevelt Library: 46c, 48tc, 48br, 49bl, 49tr. Sagamore Hill National Historic Site: 36lb, 36cb. Sherwood Forest Plantation: 18lc. Smithsonian Institution: 9la, 10c, 10b, 12ra, 13c, 14la, 14cb, 16lb, 17ra, 20rc, 20lb, 24tl, 24rb, 25lc, 27lc, 27ca, 29tl, 29bl, 29c, 29r, 30c, 30rb, 31bl, 31br, 32tl, 34tl, 34bl, 34bc, 34r, 35lb, 35c, 35r, 36ca, 36tr, 37tl, 37lc, 38c, 38ra, 39ca, 39lb, 39rb, 40tl, 40tr, 40b, 41l, 41tr, 41rc, 41br, 43tl, 44tl, 47r, 48la, 50ra, 54bl, 54tr, 55tl, 56l, 56cb, 56rb, 57lc, 58c, 58r, 59rb, 61tr, 61r, 67bl, 68cb, 70tl Eric Long. Sophia Smith Collection, Smith College: 24lc. United States Department of the Interior, National Park Service, Adams National Historical Park: 8l, 8rc, 8b, 9c, 15tr, 66tl. University of New Hampshire Media Center: 46l Trude Fleischmann. The White House: 58tl, 62tl. White House Collection, Courtesy White House Historical Association: 9b, 12tl, 12rb, 18lb, 28l, 36tl, 60ca. WireImage: 66cr. Woodrow Wilson House, an historic site of the National Trust for Historic Preservation in the United States: 66c.

All other images © Dorling Kindersley

For further information see:
www.dkimages.com

72